A Single Girl's ULTIMATE Bucket List

A Single Girl's ULTIMATE Bucket List

Sarah Melland

RMM
RIPE MELLAND MEDIA

Copyright © 2020 Sarah Melland
Published by Ripe Melland Media

All rights reserved. No part of this publication may be reproduced, stored in a retrieval system, or transmitted, in any form or by any means, electronic, mechanical, photocopying, recording, or otherwise, without the prior written permission of the publisher.

ISBN: 978-1-7346333-3-7

Front Cover Design by Sara Mason
www.saramason.wordpress.com

Contents

Introduction	1
Travel Tips	2
How to Make Money While Traveling	13
Travel Around the World	18
Books to Read	127
Movies to Watch	136
Dating... Mating... Procreating	150
...And Everything in-between	174
Food, Booze, Wine & Dine	213
Be One with Nature	235
References	250

Introduction

For anyone who ponders the meaning of life, here is a quick tip: Life is what you make of it. And to accompany you on your journey, here is your ultimate bucket list. It will travel with you through all life's amazing adventures. No experience is too big or small; You will collect amazing memories from all of them. If there is one thing I wish I would have realized in my twenties, it's how much I love to travel, (I didn't get a passport until I was 29…) and I regret that I didn't start sooner. This is why I am passing all this information onto you. It's so you won't have regrets, and will get to experience everything life has to offer.

I have tried to include everything I think you would need to make your traveling dreams come true, including hacks, tips and ways to make money while seeing the world.

The biggest advice I can give you is to get out of your comfort zone as much as possible. I know you want to stay in your shit and be scared, but don't miss out on opportunities by continuing to think that way. Just go and do it. Once you do, you will realize it wasn't so bad. The more you break through the fear, the easier it becomes. Embrace your nerves, because they'll never go away.

Let go of your inhibitions when you travel and get to know yourself and what you like. Take a page from Chelsea Handler's book *My Horizontal Life:* Give yourself a fake name for the night and pretend to be a completely different persona.

Expect everything to go wrong, or better yet, don't have any expectations at all. Also, don't get upset if something does go wrong. It will all work out the way it was supposed to. Trust me, my second day in Thailand, my phone got destroyed and I had to spend two weeks disconnected from the world. It was the most glorious thing that could have happened to me.

Here are some quick little insights on traveling that didn't fit anywhere else in this bucket list book. Always, no matter what, keep an open mind. You never know what is around the corner or what life has to offer. You might not know you like something if you don't try it. Have I got all the cliché things to write about living your best life yet? Basic AF? Good, who cares. Sorry not sorry. K. Thanks. Bye.

Be patient. Things will work out in the end. No need to rush. You'll get to where you are going in due time. Travel is about the journey, not the destination. Be respectful. Locals are often willing to help you out, but there might be a language barrier so keep your cool when something doesn't go your way. If you don't, you'll end up just looking like an asshole-y tourist.

Travel Tips

I will admit I got a lot of these great tips from travel bloggers, who have a ton of different travel articles if you are serious about seeing the world and want to check them out. I will leave my favorites in the reference section. If you are already a travel pro, you can skip this, but it's always a good refresher and you might learn something new.

Before Your Trip

- ❖ **Write down the address of your accommodation before you arrive.** Put it everywhere so you don't forget. Literally everywhere, I did not do this in Thailand, and really wish I would have, especially since I didn't speak the language.

- ❖ **Go for several test walks with your packed backpack.** It'll likely be much heavier than you think. This will really help you narrow down the essentials to bring, and decide what to leave behind.

- ❖ **Give family/friends copies of your itinerary.** From a safety perspective, it's good to have several people back home who know where you'll be. Forward any flight and accommodation confirmations to your family. Also check in with them periodically.

- ❖ **Save early and bring more money than you think you'll need.** It's good to have a budget to stick to, but most people tend to go over.

- ❖ **Get your phone unlocked before you leave.** With an unlocked phone, you'll be able to buy local SIM cards and access cheap data as you travel. Cheap data means getting to use Google Maps when you're lost.

- ❖ **Invest in a good camera.** Your photos will be a record of some of your best memories, so invest in a good camera. Before your trip, watch YouTube tutorials on how to use it like a semi-pro. Maybe even take some photography classes.

- ❖ **Scan important documents and email them to yourself.** Scan a copy of your passport, visas, and debit/credit cards you're traveling with. Password-protect the documents, and email a copy to yourself and to a family member. If everything you own gets stolen, you can access them safely from your email account and take the copies to your embassy to prove you are who you say you are.

- ❖ **Read up about local customs before you go.** You don't want to offend anyone while you travel, so make sure you're aware of any inappropriate gestures or behavior before you arrive.

- ❖ **Check your passport's expiration date.** You won't be able to travel if you have less than six months' validity on your passport!

Health

- ❖ **Have a health checkup before you leave.** Visit your doctor and dentist for a checkup before your trip. The last thing you want is to set off and discover two weeks later that you need to get a tooth filled in some random country. Also, find out about any necessary shots you might need or certain medications you should bring.

- ❖ **Wear sunscreen every day.** As a tanning expert, please, please do this! You have no idea how much damage you will do to your skin, especially in tropical locations as they tend to have an extremely high UV index. Trust me, I have seen middle-aged women who look fabulous and others whose skin is torn up. Don't be the latter.

- ❖ **Eat healthier every now and then.** I know it's hard in a foreign country when they don't always have the best options, but try at least once a day. You want to get nutrients since you will be walking around a lot. Make sure to have some sort of veggie or fruit in every meal.

- ❖ **Drink more water.** It's easy to get caught up and forget, but regardless, always drink water. Your skin will love you. You can also pack a collapsible water bottle so it doesn't take up room in your bag.

- ❖ **Carry a basic first-aid kit.** Accidents happen, so be prepared. I take band-aids, antibacterial cream, and ointments for minor cuts and scrapes. Not to mention if you get bug bites. I was miserable in Thailand, so remember to pack bug spray as well.

- ❖ **Treat your body well.** Remember to be nice to your body in general. Get enough sleep, stay hydrated, eat healthily, use sunscreen and exercise often.

Culture

- ❖ **Learn a few words of the language in every country you visit.** You'll gain more respect from the locals, especially if you know how to be polite by saying 'please' and 'thank you,' for example. Remember: if you don't speak the language, it's your problem, not theirs. And please don't start speaking louder to make yourself understood. Try miming instead, or using a translation app on your phone. Also, be courteous and smile often! Don't forget this.

- ❖ **The best activities aren't necessarily traditional tourist ones.** My favorite memory was meeting a local bartender in Chiang Mai. She talked to us about everything and even wanted to braid my hair. It was girl talk at its finest, and we learned that they have to deal with the same shit with men that we do back home.

- ❖ **Say yes to random invitations.** Again, no regrets. It is the best thing you can do and the best time you will ever have. Trust me. I met a gorgeous man who took me on the time of my life. As always though, make sure you are safe and have someone with you. Be careful and take extra safety precautions.

- ❖ **Eat the local food.** I don't care if you are picky eater, you can at least try something once to decide. If not, you will live a sad life not experiencing the local food and learning about the culture. Also visit the local markets. Try the strange foods, even insects! You have to say you did it, you just have to. No regrets.

- ❖ **Always visit the local tourism office.** They know about everything going on in town. They can point you to free activities, special events happening during your stay, and everything in between. They even offer discounts on attractions and transportation.

- ❖ **Ask hostel staff for information.** Hostel staff deal with budget travelers every day. They know exactly where you should go for cheap meals and attractions. They also tend to be locals so they know the city. Even if you aren't staying in a hostel, just pop in and ask for help.

- ❖ **Read a history book.** You can't understand a place's present if you don't know anything about its past. Read up on the destinations you are visiting. It will give you a deeper understanding the culture.

- ❖ **Don't be afraid of other countries.** The news media loves to report on tourists getting kidnapped or killed. However, the world is not nearly as dangerous as the media makes it out to be. Keep an eye out for sketchy situations, but don't let that be the focus of your whole trip. It is a good idea to check out what's going on in an area before you visit, as well as what areas to stay away from.

Advice

- ❖ **Take more photos of yourself.** Don't be shy, you will regret it if you don't embrace the camera. Trust me, there are pictures I took on my trips that I wish I would have been in. The scenery was beautiful and now it just looks like a gorgeous photo that someone else took, like I wasn't there. Don't be me, be better.

- ❖ **Bring ear plugs and a sleep mask.** These are needed if you are traveling on a budget and staying in hostels or dorm rooms. They also are useful on airplanes.

- **Space saver bags will help you fit more in your backpack.** You throw your clothes in, seal the bag, then roll it up to push out all the air.

- **Bring several debit and credit cards with you.** Bring at least three debit/credit cards with you that are all linked to different accounts, and don't keep them all in the same place in case you get robbed or leave one somewhere. Accidents happen and you never want to be without money in a foreign country.

- **Bring a stash of emergency cash.** Don't forget to also split this up as well. Most bloggers I have seen keep it around 300 US dollars. It is up to you how much you want to bring. Also, when you go out, take only what you need. Limit the amount of cash and bank cards you carry with you, so if something does happen, you can easily recover.

- **Back up everything in multiple places.** Imagine how you'd feel if you lost every single photo from your trip. You really don't want that to happen, so back everything up, in multiple places.

- **Have a routine when checking out of a place.** It would be horrible to forget your passport. Make a checklist. Check every nook, cranny, closet and drawer twice.

- **Let your bank know you'll be traveling.** Along with notifying your credit card companies. Tell them when you are going, what cities you are traveling to and all that jazz. You don't want your card getting shut down for an unbeknownst reason.

- **If you are not sure if you should bring it, don't.** When in doubt, leave it behind. You don't want to be carrying around clothes in your luggage from place to place that you aren't sure you are going to wear. Always bring comfortable easy clothes and amazing walking shoes.

- **Don't be shamed into not buying souvenirs.** I love getting museum books and picture frames. My girlfriend collects shot glasses. Have fun with your souvenir. You will be glad you did.

- **Use a VPN.** You'll be connecting to a whole range of unsecured Wi-Fi networks on your trip, so you need to use a VPN to protect yourself from hackers and malware. A VPN, or Virtual Private Network, is a private network that encrypts and transmits data while it travels from one place to another on the internet. Using a VPN to connect to the internet allows you to surf websites privately and securely as well as gain access to restricted websites and overcome censorship blocks.

- **Solid toiletries are the best.** Especially if you want to travel carry-on only. They have shampoos, conditioners, sunscreen and insect repellent that come in solid form. These will be easier to travel with and not make such a mess if spilled.

- **Get a travel towel.** Travel towels are quick-drying, incredibly lightweight, and fold up so small! You never know when you will need it, whether it's at the beach, on a picnic, or just to dry off.

- **Don't change your currency at the airport.** That's where you'll get the worst exchange rates.

- **Wear flip-flops in the hostel showers.** Same with dorm rooms! You don't want to get warts. Gross!

- **Always pack your things the night before your early morning flight.** Trust me, you don't want to wake up the next morning hungover and realize you missed your train, and that you have thirty minutes to get to your next one or you will miss your flight. I may or may not have done that. Ah, Paris.

- **Keep a journal.** Keep a journal to remember those small details about things that happen to you because you'll treasure them in future years. The journal I recommend? THIS one! You are welcome, ladies :) If you don't want to lug around this bad boy, find a smaller one to keep notes in.

- **Wear your normal clothes.** You don't have to buy apparel specifically for traveling that has breathable material and all the zippers and pockets. I never get that fancy, plus they are ugly. Not to mention, you stand out like a sore thumb.

- **Go to the places that interest you most.** What do you feel most drawn to? What places are at the top of your list and go there first. Also, accept that you won't be able to see everything.

- **Google Translate is so incredibly helpful.** Download the Google Translate app before you leave and use the camera feature for translating menus, signs, posters, and anything else you need to read.

- **Travel with a toilet roll.** Grab half a roll, squash it up, and keep it in a sandwich bag with you. Trust me…Trust me! I'll spare you the hellish details.

- **Use HERE Maps for offline navigation.** Don't have data? You can download entire country maps through HERE Maps and get walking directions for anywhere you need to go.

- **A power strip will make charging easy.** Bring a power strip to ensure you can charge what you need to, while allowing everyone else to charge their tech, too. Also, don't forget outlet converters.

- **A dry bag is more useful than you think.** When you are on a boat, or at the Songkran Festival in Thailand. These are a must to keep your electronics safe and belongings. Just don't forget to put your stuff back in them.

- **Be skeptical of TripAdvisor reviews.** The same goes with Yelp, we went on Yelp for great restaurants and were let down. Take recommendations from locals whenever possible and maybe the concierge at the hotel.

- **Charge your devices whenever you have the chance.** You should also have a backup battery for your phone. When you see a spare socket, charge it. You don't want to run out of juice on the top of the Eiffel Tower.

- **Protect your technology.** Get water proof cases for everything in case a coffee spills on your laptop. You can never be too careful. Waterproof case for your phone as well, as I think I have told you why this is important.

- **Pack contraception.** You don't want the biggest souvenir from your trip to be an STD or a baby. Pack contraception, and have safe sex. My girlfriend packed a mega box for our trip to Europe, just to be on the safe side.

- **Find photogenic spots with Instagram.** Follow local Instagrammers in the places you'll be visiting to find the best spots for taking photos. Search hashtags relating to the places to check out the popular photos and see where they were taken.

- **Make a playlist for memories.** I wish I would have thought of this when our Uber driver in Paris, was telling us all the amazing sex songs they had in France. Yes, we asked him to play them for us, and yes, we were inebriated.

- **Take into account jetlag and travel fatigue.** This is in travel blogs, but I have never had jetlag going to places, but not saying you won't. A good travel trip is you have to trick your brain. Trust me, it has worked every time. Just know whatever time that's what time it is. The only problem was when I came home from London, I was a little topsy turvy for two days.

- **Track your spending.** You don't want to run out of money on day four of a thirteen-day trip.

- **Pack light.** It's OK to wear the same t-shirt a few days in a row. Take half the clothes you think you will need…you won't need as much as you think.

- **Always get behind business travelers when in security lines.** They move fast since they are usually in a rush and travel light. They know the drill. Never get behind families. They take forever.

- **Pack a flashlight.** You never know when you might need it, especially in the middle of the night.

- **Observe daily life around you.** If you really want to get a feel for the pulse of a place, spend a few hours sitting in a park or on a busy street corner watching the day-to-day life happen in front of you. The smells, the colors, human interactions, and sounds. It's a kind of meditation.

- **Bring an extra camera battery.** You don't ever want to miss out on a photo opportunity because your camera died. Also, don't forget to charge it when you get back to your hotel. Don't know if I have said this already, but it is worth repeating, bring an extra memory card.

Tourist Traps

- **The smaller the menu, the better the restaurant.** That's why street food is so delicious! If you skip the street food, you miss out on culture. While you're traveling, look for places that only do a handful of dishes rather than offering 500 options. Ask for recommendations.

- **Travel in "shoulder season" to save money and avoid crowds.** It is the travel period between peak and off-peak season.

- **Get up early.** Arrive early for everything and you'll get to experience major attractions at their least busy times.

- **Lunchtime is the best time to visit historical sites.** You'll have fewer crowds getting in your way as big tour buses, groups, and most travelers head to lunch. It's always best to visit an attraction super early, late, or when people eat.

- **Never eat in a touristy area or near a tourist attraction.** As a general rule, walk five blocks in either direction before finding a place to eat. The closer you are to tourist attractions, the more you are going to pay and the worse the food will be. Additionally, never eat where the menu is in six languages! That means the restaurant is just for tourists.

- **Eat at expensive restaurants during lunch.** Most expensive restaurants offer lunch specials featuring the same food they would serve for dinner but at half the price!

- **Take pictures of your luggage and clothes.** If your bag gets lost, this will help identify it more easily and speed up the process of having your travel insurance reimburse you.

Safety

- **Don't put anything in your back pockets.** This should be a duh! But it has to be said, since people are stupid.

- **Always carry a padlock.** They come in handy, especially when you stay in dorms and need to secure your stuff. Carry a small combination lock with you when you travel. Don't use one with keys because if you lose the keys, you're screwed! Also, this is obvious but never bring valuables with you while traveling.

- **Write down emergency info.** If disaster strikes, you might not have time to search for numbers for local police or ambulance services, or directions to the nearest embassy for your country. Create an "Emergency Plan" for you to follow if things turn disastrous. Save it on your phone.

- **Check the state department website.** The U.S. Department of State has a page for every country in the world where it lists all known difficulties and current threats. Advice is generally on the hyper-cautious side. Warnings will give you a general idea of what's going on in the country you're visiting, and specific problem areas you may want to avoid.

❖ **Ask locals for advice.** If you really want to know which neighborhoods are safe and which might be sketchy, ask a local resident of the area. Don't be afraid to ask them which parts of the city to avoid and how much taxi fares should cost (this is a big one).

❖ **Register with your embassy.** The Smart Traveler Enrollment Program, from the U.S. Department of State, is designed to make a destination's local embassy aware of your arrival and keep you constantly updated with the latest safety information. It's free and a great way to get reliable up-to-date safety information as you travel, along with giving you an extra level of security in case of emergencies. That way if something happens, like a natural disaster or terrorist attack, the local embassy can get a hold of you quickly to share important information or help with evacuation.

❖ **Don't share too much with strangers.** If you're ever tempted to make your itinerary more public, like with a Facebook post, just remember it can be used as a roadmap of your movements. Don't share too many details about your travel plans or accommodation details with people you've just met. Be vague about an area of town rather than the name of your hotel. Sharing that you're new might also signal you're a good target for scams.

❖ **Be aware of your clothing.** When it comes to travel, the wrong clothes scream "TOURIST" and can make you a target for scammers, thieves and worse. The less you look like an obvious visitor, the less attention you'll get from the wrong kind of people. Wearing the right clothes is also a sign of respect. Ignoring local customs can come across as both arrogant and ignorant. In conservative countries, it's just safer to dress more conservatively yourself. Start by checking out Wikipedia's general advice on clothing laws by country.

❖ **Splurge on extra safety.** Sometimes it's worth the extra few bucks to splurge on a slightly better hostel, a more convenient flight, a taxi home from the bar, or a tour operator with a strong safety record.

❖ **Stay "tethered" to your bag.** Keep your bag tethered to something immovable at all times, and do so in a really obvious way. Thieves will consider it way too risky a job – and will leave you alone.

❖ **Learn basic self-defense.** You don't need black-belt skills, but taking a few self-defense classes is a worthwhile investment in your personal safety. A great way to neutralize a threat is to get yourself as far away as physically possible. If someone with a gun or knife just wants your phone, give it to them, run away, and live another day. Use force only when your life is threatened and there are absolutely no other options available.

❖ **Project situational awareness.** Did you know that a majority of human communication is based on non-verbal body language? This projection of confidence can prevent you from becoming a target. Keep your head up, stay alert and remain aware of your surroundings. When you're confident, potential attackers can sense it through your body language and eye contact.

❖ **Use ATMs wisely.** You may have been told to cover your hand when keying in your PIN number at an ATM. Always take a close look at ATM machines before you use them too. Pull on the card reader a bit. Does it have any questionable signs of tampering? If so, go into the bank and get someone to come out and check it. If an ATM machine appears to have eaten your card, run a finger along the card slot to see if you feel anything protruding. The "Lebanese Loop" is a trick thieves use where a thin plastic sleeve captures your card (preventing the machine from reading it) – then as soon as you walk away, a thief yanks out the reader and runs off with your card. Another overlooked factor is where other people are when you're at the machine. Can someone peer over your shoulder? Are they close enough to be able to grab your cash and run off? If so, use another ATM elsewhere. Better safe than sorry! Never let anyone "help" you with your transaction either.

❖ **Travel in numbers.** The more people around you, the more eyeballs are on your valuables – and the more legs are available for running after thieves. A group is also a much more intimidating physical presence, which helps ward off predators of all kinds. If you're traveling solo, consider making some new friends and go exploring together. Staying at backpacker hostels is an excellent way to make some new friends. Don't leave your expensive or important stuff with someone you just met though, no matter how friendly they seem.

❖ **Stay (relatively) sober.** Getting too drunk or high when you travel is almost always unacceptably risky. Stay hyper-aware of how much you're consuming, keep hydrated, fed, and make sure you don't lose control of the situation.

❖ **Trust your instincts!** You are a walking surveillance network. Your body sees and hears more things than you could ever translate into coherent thought. Your body might sense signs of danger before your brain is fully aware. This is why gut feelings are always worth examining! If you're feeling uneasy and you don't know why, try not to write it off as irrational fear. Stop and pay closer attention to the situation.

Travel Hacks

❖ **Travel slow to save money.** You can negotiate long-term stays at your accommodation to save money per night.

❖ **Make the most of your layovers.** Try to get a 24-hour or 48-hour layover whenever you can. You can get another mini vacation out of it and see some more places!

❖ **Use an incognito browser window to book everything.** It's a window that doesn't store your browsing history on your computer. You can use it when booking flights or making accommodations. Sometimes prices will gradually increase for flights as you keep checking them, but will drop if you use an incognito browser.

❖ **Take advantage of your youth.** If you're under 25, there are a whole heap of student discounts you can use to your advantage. You can get cheaper flights through STA Travel, cheaper train passes through Eurail, free access to museums and more. Always check to see if student discounts are available before booking anything.

❖ **Make sure to use no-fee bank cards.** Get a credit card and debit card that doesn't charge a foreign transaction fee or an ATM fee. Over the course of a long trip, the few dollars they take every time will really add up! Especially at $2.75 a pop or more.

❖ **Don't fly direct.** When booking flights, sometimes it is cheaper to fly into airports close to your final destination, and then take a train or bus to where you need to go. Be sure to shop around for your flight and know that direct isn't always the cheapest route.

❖ **One-way tickets are better than roundtrip.** It gives you the freedom to be spontaneous.

❖ **Mark your luggage so it stands out.** Put some stickers on it, some duct tape along one side or tie some ribbons to the handle. Be creative, use whatever your little heart desires.

❖ **When you check in to the hotel, don't be afraid to ask for an upgrade.** Hotels have a lot of flexibility when it comes to assigning upgrades at check-in. It never hurts to ask. Often times they can accommodate you if the hotel isn't full. Just be super nice! You are living your best life right now. Anything is possible. I got upgraded to the presidential suite at The Venetian in Vegas one time. Glad I inquired!

❖ **Book flights 2-3 months in advance to get the best price.** Don't waste five hours searching and trying to save ten bucks on flight.

❖ **Stay in hostels.** They are cheap, and some even have private rooms. I have only stayed in the private rooms, not the ones with multiple people in one room. I am all about being safe. So really research before you commit to a group room. In general, staying in hostels instead of hotels will save you hundreds.

❖ **Use Meetup, the sharing economy and hospitality websites to meet locals.** These websites will help you get an insider's perspective on your destination by connecting you with locals in the places you visit.

❖ **Avoid taxis.** They are always a budget buster. Never, ever take a taxi unless you absolutely have too. In London though, I might recommend the actual taxis there as the drivers went to school for their profession and know the city in detail. Most London locals told us to not take Uber or Lyft as they are not as safe.

❖ **Take an empty metal water bottle through airport security and fill it up at your gate.** Drink from the tap when you can. If you're going somewhere where you can't drink the unfiltered tap water, be sure to get a water bottle with a filter.

❖ **Take free walking tours.** These tours will give you a good orientation and background of the city you are visiting.

❖ **Get city attraction cards.** If you are going to visit a lot of museums and other attractions in a short period of time, a city pass is going to save you money on admission and free public transportation. A word to the wise, first map out what you are going to do. I don't feel we got our money's worth when we bought one in Paris because we weren't efficient with our planning.

❖ **Learn to haggle.** Haggling is a fun, playful way of not getting charged the foreigner price. It's the art of negotiating and one that will help you throughout all of life, not just at the market.

❖ **Use points and miles for free travel.** You can go a lot further in the world when you don't have to pay for it. Learn the art of travel hacking and collect points and miles through your everyday spending so you can get free flights. There is a definite art to this travel hack. I would read up on this and how people do it if you are seriously interested.

❖ **Book your tickets online.** If you're planning to do any activities or excursions on your trip, book them online. Companies usually offer a discounted price online compared to buying in person. Not only that, but you'll be able to pay with a credit card, giving you some extra protection as well as more travel points.

❖ **Sign up for flight deals.** When it comes to travel, your flights will likely be your biggest expense. Save money by signing up for airline deal websites like Scott's Cheap Flights, The Flight Deal, and Secret Flying. If you have the time and they have overbooked the flight and are offering free travel vouchers, take them. You usually arrive only a few hours later.

❖ **Avoid expensive hotels & resorts.** You're never in your room except to sleep and shower. It's stupid to waste money on extremely expensive hotels. Although, we did splurge on a hotel when we went to Paris. Worth it! Let your hair down every once and awhile.

❖ **Claim Compensation for Your Disrupted Flight.** The more you fly, the more likely you are to experience a flight disruption. This annoying occurrence might earn you up to a few hundred dollars, provided that you arrive at your final destination at least three hours later than the scheduled time of arrival. The alternative is to entrust Claim Compass with your claim. Claim Compass is a platform that lets you file a claim with an airline quickly and efficiently.

HOW TO MAKE MONEY WHILE TRAVELING

I am going to warn you, don't think these tips will make you a millionaire. But if you dip your hand in a lot of honey pots at once, you could potentially make a good passive income.

- **Rent your car.** The best personal vehicle rental service out there is provided by Turo. You can set a minimum price for trips and they'll fill your fuel tank for you when you come back. Your car is protected up to one million dollars, covered against theft and damage, and it's totally free to list it!

- **Rent your home.** You might have friends or friends of friends looking for a place to stay while you're on the road. In this case, it's settled. Otherwise, use Airbnb's platform to lend your home to a stranger. It will come with a one-million-dollar insurance policy just like your car rental.

- **Rent your home out as a filming location.** If you are in Los Angeles or a place that has a lot of shoots for commercials, movies, tv shows or anything else, you can sign up for people to film at your residence.

- **Sell goods online.** You can buy and sell pretty much anything online. It can be things you found during your trip. If you're traveling to cheap countries, consider shopping around small markets for hand-made products and then sell them online. Put what you craft by yourself up for sale! EBay is still a good option. Set up your own website or open a shop on an already popular platform that registers more traffic, like Amazon.

- **Sell your photos and videos.** There are tons of stock images websites online that will pay you for your best shots like Adobe Stock, Shutterstock or Foap. However, find out how much they pay for a download because it's usually only a few cents. That's why I wouldn't put all my efforts on this one if you're not ready to spend some serious time to improve your photography skills.

- **Publish an eBook.** Write about something you know very well or even fiction! Maximize your chances of generating sales by creating an eBook on a niche topic that isn't too competitive. Once your eBook is written, publish it and promote it. Remember it's passive income so you probably won't make a ton right away, but you will constantly get residuals if your eBook does relatively well.

- **Become an Influencer.** During your travels, you will need equipment: clothing, gear, transportation. How about contacting brands providing these and offering to be ambassadors for them? Ambassadors usually get fifty percent off. They will be more inclined to sign a deal with you if you already boast a decent audience on social media. Consider contacting smaller brands who need exposure just as much as you. They'll be easier to convince. Some of the most popular platforms that will put you on the path to becoming an opinion leader include IZEA, FameBit and OpenInfluence. Find a niche, because again it is oversaturated. It goes without saying that it requires a ton of work and that you don't become an influencer overnight.

- **Get paid for living a healthy life.** Download the Pact app. Pact is a program whose aim is to help you keep your word on your weight loss journey. You make a pact with yourself and stay connected to a community on the app that ensures you will uphold that pledge. You get money every time you stick to your exercise goals and lose money when you don't. Don't expect to earn a fortune, but it's perfect to buy yourself a free meal from time to time

- **Flower, vegetable and fruit picking.** Seasonal work has become a very popular option for travelers unafraid of getting their hands dirty, particularly in Australia. Use indeed.com and type "seasonal" or "fruit" in the keywords of your search along with your destination. Consider also doing a direct Google search like "fruit picking jobs in [country]". You might end up finding a local website with interesting offers.

- **Bars/Restaurants.** Working in bars and restaurants is perhaps the most popular sort of seasonal work worldwide. Even better if you have a working holiday visa. If you don't, you can always find an owner who's ready to pay you under the table. Before heading to the manager and ask for a job, make sure you learn the basics of the local language.

- **Resort or summer camp work.** Beautiful locations around the world are often the promised lands for resorts and summer camp organizations taking advantage of the pleasant climate and environment to build a business. They need people at the front desk, the kitchen, cleaning the property, and you could also consider being a lifeguard or part of the activity team! Check out jobmonkey.com for job offers online.

- **House-Sitting.** In exchange for looking after someone else's house (and maybe their pets as well), you get to stay at their place for free! There are several websites that can put you in touch with owners looking for someone to keep an eye on their house such as mindmyhouse.com and trustedhousesitters.com.

- **Hostels.** Some new staff is often needed even just for a few hours. In exchange for taking care of the front desk or cleaning, you can expect at least a free lodging. Check out workinhostels.com or simply go ask them if they need help for the day or during the week.

- **Model.** Particularly in countries where you stand out from the crowd, you might get asked to model. Abroad, when you look different from the locals, you are perceived as exotic. Use that to your advantage! You can inquire at the local modeling agencies.

- **Volunteer work.** Most places offer housing and food for your help. There are several websites to find volunteer work, one of them being grassrootvolunteering.org.

- **Work exchange programs.** Choose where you want to go, check out the offers available, contact the host and if you're accepted, book your cheap flight and go work while traveling! The most popular organizations are HelpX, WWOOF, and Worldpackers.

- **Freelancing.** The option praised by many digital travelers is to become a freelancer in any industry that allows it. Set up a profile on some of the most popular platforms, Upwork and Fiverr. Try to start while you are not yet traveling, to build references and earn some money before your departure. Check out nomadlist.com as well as Facebook groups. You'll find plenty of useful tips and support there.

    - **Web designers and programmers.** Browse through skillshare.com to find something you'd like to learn. You can start with codeacademy.com to get started with programming.

    - **Writer, translator and transcriptionist.** You can offer to guest post on large online platforms if your writing skills allow it. There are also tons of opportunities to become a translator or transcriptionist. Speak at least 2 languages? You should find something. More than 4? You will for sure.

    - **Marketing and social media manager.** There are blog posts released every day for so many companies that struggle to stand out from the crowd due to lack of experience in marketing. If you've got a good understanding of how SEO works, this would be good for you. The same goes for managing social media accounts.

    - **Consulting.** Small businesses are often on the lookout for experts to get advice on their business plan or to assist them in their product launch. With experience in the startup environment or in consulting in general, you should discover tons of companies seeking help.

- **Small jobs.** There are a ton of jobs you can do while traveling for some extra cash. For example, website or app tester. You can do this from pretty much anywhere as long as you have software to record your screen and a microphone. Again, indeed.com and upwork.com gather many offers for website and app testing. Taking online surveys is another idea. However, lot of these are bullshit scams that take and sell your info to third parties so be wary and Google them before you sign up. Many companies organize online surveys to test a product or understand what would be the most appropriate marketing strategy for the release. You could also apply to become a survey taker on a platform like mysurvey.com. Jackson Consumer Testing is another one, which is based in the US.

- **Travel blogger.** Or any type of blogger for that matter. Before reaching the point where you can travel around as much as you want and get paid for it, you will have to put in a lot of work. You need to get a decent amount of traffic to monetize your content. One way to do it is through affiliate marketing: add links to your content redirecting clickers to a page where they can buy something. If they do purchase the item after clicking through your link, you get a commission. You can strike such deals with Amazon, Awin or Bluehost for instance.

- **Affiliate marketing.** Making money this way is definitely possible even though the competition can be high. But if you're willing to dedicate yourself to a couple of months' worth of research, you'll find your niche and hopefully a steady paycheck. If you don't know much about affiliate marketing, have a look at affilorama.com, which offers an excellent series of free lessons.

❖ **Flight attendant.** This job is perhaps the one that most embodies the idea of traveling to make a living. Apply for job openings on airline websites and get ready to ace the interviews and tests, because the competition will be tough!

❖ **Tour escort.** Making a career as a tour escort also guarantees you traveling around on a regular basis. Guide groups of tourists around their destination, show them the best places to eat, visit and have fun. The salary usually isn't that fantastic, but you do make a modest living and travel at the same time. Find tour escort jobs in agencies at your destination or online, via indeed.com for example.

❖ **Cruise ship.** Check out allcrusiejobs.com to get an idea of what kind of positions are available. Head for the Caribbean, that's where most travelers find their first job on a boat. After that, it gets easier because you will build a network very quickly once you're in.

❖ **Yacht or sailboat.** Boat owners are sometimes looking for an additional pair of hands to help them out on board. It's a great way to learn more about sailing or simply get a free ride somewhere. Findacrew.net is a very popular platform that puts you in touch with boat owners looking for people to join them.

❖ **Traveling show.** If you have any kind of talent, either as a singer, dancer, or even entertainer this is for you. Joining a circus, band, show, or theater troupe is sure to leave you with amazing stories to tell, in addition to cash in your pocket. You might also join them as a photographer or maybe even manager if you have the skills!

❖ **Teaching.** With udemy.com and takelessons.com you can offer to teach pretty much anything.

❖ **Languages.** The cool part is that even without certifications, it's very simple to find a job as a language teacher. If you do have certifications, you might even get hired by official institutions. With WhatsApp, Hangout, and Skype, it's super easy to communicate no matter where you are in the world! You can be a teacher and earn money traveling overseas very easily. Dave's ESL Cafe (eslcafe.com) is popular to find such a job. But you can also earn money by teaching languages online once you've set up a profile on upwork.com for instance.

❖ **Musical instruments.** You can set up a YouTube channel for your musical instrument tutorial videos and work to attract followers. Many YouTubers earn a living with their videos, which can be a full-time job. For some quick money though, takelessons.com is a better option.

❖ **Dancing and singing.** You can make dancing or singing tutorials or do the job in person.

❖ **Yoga.** Teaching yoga around the world is a trend that's gaining in popularity worldwide!

❖ **Surfing.** Surfing attracts tons of beginners whose dream is simply to be able to stand on a board. A lot of instructors at the beach do it part-time. There are countless surfing spots worldwide. You can easily travel to the best places on earth and teach how to surf there.

- ❖ **Scuba-diving.** Advertise on divezone.net if you haven't picked your destination yet: if someone is interested in your profile, book your flight and head there! Find a scuba-diving center and ask if they need a new person to help with the newbies.

- ❖ **Movie extra.** You can reach out to local agencies organizing castings. It is not glamorous however. The hours are usually long and they may not use you at all.

- ❖ **Day-trading.** If you like to travel light, you might be willing to get rid of some of your possessions along the way. Consider trading them for money rather than just throwing them away. I've always been inspired by the story of this guy, Kyle MacDonald, who started off with a paperclip and ended up with a house, just by trading upward for more and more valuable items.

- ❖ **Upload local job flyers.** Snap a picture of a job flyer that you come across while walking on the street and upload it to Job Spotter. You won't get cash per se, but you will be rewarded with an Amazon gift card.

- ❖ **Edit menus and signs.** The signs were written in English, Spanish and French in addition to Chinese. During your trips abroad, you will probably come upon weirdly spelled or grammatically intriguing signs: take a picture as a souvenir and offer to correct it!

- ❖ **Trading stock options.** Another way to make money online consists of trading in the stock exchange. If you know your way around it and already have money on the side waiting to be invested, you can make real money very quickly. The riskier the investment, the bigger the potential return.

- ❖ **Sell timeshares.** If you were born to be a salesperson, then head to Greece, Thailand, Mexico, the Caribbean or any other major resort area and you can find work selling timeshares. The earning potential is huge in this line of work.

- ❖ **Join an MLM or social media retail.** An MLM is a multi-level marketing platform. Some are great, some are not so great. So do your research. And make sure you believe in the product and what you are selling. I have seen a lot of ones with beauty products, clothing, and nails.

- ❖ **Sell your art & crafts at local markets.** There are markets in many places where foreigners can rent a stall and sell their goods. Or sell your art online. The best platforms are society6.com, redbubble.com, or threadless.com.

Travel Around the World

Africa

Democratic Republic of the Congo

☐ **Virunga National Park.** You will have a chance to get a close encounter with the highly endangered Mountain Gorilla. I am pretty sure every Gorilla movie is set here including *Congo* and *Mighty Joe Young*. I would love to have a pet Gorilla. I would also love to learn sign language. Ironically enough, the best time to enjoy clear blue skies (particularly for photography purposes) is during the rainy months (April, May, October and November), as it can get quite foggy during the dry season.

Date Completed: _____

Zambia

☐ **Shower in Victoria Falls.** Also known as "The Smoke That Thunders." If you are feeling adventurous, there are rafting tours, or you can do a scenic helicopter ride. However, if you decide to see it, it will be magically breathtaking. The best time to visit the spectacular Victoria Falls is from February to May, directly after the region's summer rains, when you'll see the world's largest sheet of falling water flowing at its greatest volume.

Date Completed: _____

South Africa

☐ **Cape Town.** With beautiful beaches, botanical gardens and mountains, what can't you do in Cape town? The best times to visit Cape Town are from March to May and from September to November. These shoulder seasons boast enviable weather, fewer crowds, and lower prices.

Date Completed: _____

☐ **Table Mountain.** Table Mountain is a flat-topped mountain forming a prominent landmark overlooking the city of Cape Town in South Africa. It is a significant tourist attraction, with many visitors using the cableway or hiking to the top.

Date Completed: _____

Place I Visited _____

About the Culture
_____
_____
_____
_____
_____

What I Learned
_____
_____
_____
_____
_____

My Reflection
_____
_____
_____
_____
_____

A Treasured Memory
_____
_____
_____
_____
_____

A Treasured Memory
_____
_____
_____
_____
_____

Egypt

☐ **The Great Pyramids at Giza.** This is one of the Seven Wonders of the World. Also, you obviously need to see the Sphinx along with these. I would highly recommend going inside the pyramids as well to see how they were built and to marvel at how the hell they have stood the test of time. Weather-wise, the best time to visit Egypt is from October to April, as these months have pleasant temperatures. December and January are peak tourist season, so sights like the Pyramids of Giza along with the Temples of Luxor and Abu Simbel are notoriously crowded. Fun fact: Did you know the pyramids are within 1cm of true North? That's insane.
Date Completed: _____

☐ **The Nile River.** Obviously, you need to visit the longest river in the world and obviously you need to float down it in a canoe, or tube, or whatever you use to lazily drift down the stream. Corny joke coming in: Denial just ain't a river in Egypt, stated once by the great Mark Twain.
Date Completed: _____

☐ **The Great Sphinx.** A limestone statue of a reclining sphinx, a mythical creature with the body of a lion and the head of a human.
Date Completed: _____

☐ **White Desert National Park.** You'll feel like Alice going through the looking-glass. Blinding-white chalk rock spires sprout almost supernaturally from the ground, each frost-colored lollipop licked into a surreal landscape of familiar and unfamiliar shapes by the dry desert winds.
Date Completed: _____

☐ **Amun Temple Enclosure.** Amun-Ra was the local god of Karnak (Luxor) and during the New Kingdom, when the princes of Thebes ruled Egypt, he became the preeminent state god, with a temple that reflected his status.
Date Completed: _____

☐ **Temple of Horus.** It is one of the best-preserved temples in Egypt. The temple, dedicated to the falcon god Horus, was built in the Ptolemaic period between 237 and 57 BCE.
Date Completed: _____

☐ **Great Temple of Ramses II.** Carved out of the mountain on the west bank of the Nile between 1274 and 1244 BC, this imposing main temple of the Abu Simbel complex was as much dedicated to the deified Ramses II himself as to Ra-Horakhty, Amun and Ptah. The four colossal statues of the pharaoh, which front the temple, are like gigantic sentinels watching over the incoming traffic from the south, undoubtedly designed as a warning of the strength of the pharaoh.
Date Completed: _____

Place I Visited _____

About the Culture
_____
_____
_____
_____
_____

What I Learned
_____
_____
_____
_____
_____

My Reflection
_____
_____
_____
_____
_____

A Treasured Memory
_____
_____
_____
_____
_____

A Treasured Memory
_____
_____
_____
_____
_____

Tanzania

☐ **Four Seasons Safari Lodge Serengeti.** When you are in Africa, you need to go on a Safari and this one is apparently the best. If you are on a budget however, this place is not for you. It's over a grand a day. If you are doing a rich Suga Daddy type thing then go for it. Regardless, you will need to go on a Safari on the Serengeti. The best time to visit the Serengeti National Park is in the Dry season from late June to October. This period offers the best wildlife viewing in general – with the wildebeest migration as its absolute highlight.

Date Completed: _____

☐ **Mount Kilimanjaro.** If you want to hike this you absolutely can, but you need a guide by your side. There are other great peaks to see around Kilimanjaro as well for beginners, that also offer great views. There are two distinct trekking seasons which constitute the best time to climb Kilimanjaro. They are January-March and June-October.

Date Completed: _____

☐ **Ngorongoro Crater.** It's home to the vast, volcanic Ngorongoro Crater and "big 5" game (elephant, lion, leopard, buffalo, rhino). Huge herds of wildebeests and zebras traverse its plains during their annual migration. Livestock belonging to the semi-nomadic Maasai tribe graze alongside wild animals. Hominin fossils found in the Olduvai Gorge date back millions of years. Best time to go is between June to September (when general wildlife viewing is best). It is most crowded between July to March. The fewest crowds will be between April and May. The best weather with little to no rainfall is between June to October. The worst weather and the peak of the wet season is during March and April.

Date Completed: _____

☐ **Volunteer at an orphanage.** Provide assistance to overworked local staff and help give children a brighter future. Probably the most rewarding feeling ever.

Date Completed: _____

Kenya

☐ **Giraffe Manor.** Giraffe Manor is set in 12 acres of private land within 140 acres of indigenous forest in the Langata suburb of Nairobi. One of the most fascinating things about Giraffe Manor is its resident herd of Rothschild's giraffes who may visit morning and evening, poking their long necks into the windows in the hope of a treat, before retreating to their forest sanctuary. Giraffe Manor is open all year with the exception of mid-April to mid-May, which is when they do maintenance and repairs.

Date Completed: _____

Place I Visited _____

About the Culture
_____
_____
_____
_____
_____
_____

What I Learned
_____
_____
_____
_____
_____
_____

My Reflection
_____
_____
_____
_____
_____
_____

A Treasured Memory
_____
_____
_____
_____
_____
_____

A Treasured Memory
_____
_____
_____
_____
_____
_____

Other African Countries

- ☐ Algeria
- ☐ Angola
- ☐ Benin
- ☐ Botswana
- ☐ Burkina Faso
- ☐ Burundi
- ☐ Côte d'Ivoire
- ☐ Cabo Verde
- ☐ Cameroon
- ☐ Central African Republic
- ☐ Chad
- ☐ Comoros
- ☐ Congo (Congo-Brazzaville)
- ☐ Djibouti
- ☐ Equatorial Guinea
- ☐ Eritrea
- ☐ Eswatini
- ☐ Ethiopia
- ☐ Gabon
- ☐ Gambia
- ☐ Ghana
- ☐ Guinea
- ☐ Guinea-Bissau
- ☐ Lesotho
- ☐ Liberia
- ☐ Libya
- ☐ Madagascar
- ☐ Malawi
- ☐ Mali
- ☐ Mauritania
- ☐ Mauritius
- ☐ Morocco
- ☐ Mozambique
- ☐ Namibia
- ☐ Niger
- ☐ Nigeria
- ☐ Rwanda
- ☐ Sao Tome and Principe
- ☐ Senegal
- ☐ Seychelles
- ☐ Sierra Leone
- ☐ Somalia
- ☐ South Sudan
- ☐ Sudan
- ☐ Togo
- ☐ Tunisia
- ☐ Uganda
- ☐ Zimbabwe

Places I want to see in Africa

A Treasured Memory In _____

_____
_____
_____
_____

A Treasured Memory In _____

_____
_____
_____
_____
_____

A Treasured Memory In _____

_____
_____
_____
_____

A Treasured Memory In _____

_____
_____
_____
_____

A Treasured Memory In _____

_____
_____
_____
_____

A Treasured Memory In _____

_____
_____
_____
_____

Asia

China

☐ **Great Wall of China.** The only man-made structure you can see from space! It was created 2,300 years ago to protect and consolidate territories of Chinese states and empires against various nomadic groups of the Steppe and their policies. The best time to visit the Great Wall is spring and autumn. Summer is the peak season with exhausting heat and crowds. In winter it's cold and even icy, but there are almost no crowds.
Date Completed: _____

☐ **Let go of a floating lantern.** The Lantern Festival aims to promote reconciliation, peace, and forgiveness. It's usually sometime in February. If you can't get to China for this massive festival, there are others in Hawaii and Thailand.
Date Completed: _____

☐ **Walk of Faith at Tianmen Mountain.** Also known as Heaven's Gate. Could you walk across a glass bottom on the side of a tall mountain? Because that is what this is. I wouldn't recommend looking down.
Date Completed: _____

☐ **The Forbidden City.** The former Chinese imperial palace from the Ming dynasty to the end of the Qing dynasty.
Date Completed: _____

Nepal

☐ **Climb Mount Everest.** The Earth's highest mountain above sea level towering a staggering 29,029 feet. The best time for mountaineers to climb is from April to May and from September to November, which are also the most ideal periods to visit the base camp. I just want to climb it a little bit, not the whole thing, just to say I did. If you are adventurous and a pro climber, go for it! If not, I would not recommend it.
Date Completed: _____

Tibet

☐ **Meet the Dalai Lama or a monk at the Potala Palace.** The winter palace of the Dalai Lama since the 7th century, it represents Tibetan Buddhism.
Date Completed: _____

Place I Visited _____

About the Culture
_____
_____
_____
_____
_____

What I Learned
_____
_____
_____
_____
_____

My Reflection
_____
_____
_____
_____
_____

A Treasured Memory
_____
_____
_____
_____
_____

A Treasured Memory
_____
_____
_____
_____
_____

Jordan

☐ **Petra - Ancient City.** The area around Petra has been inhabited since as early as 7,000 BC. The best time to visit Petra is during the spring and autumn months, as temperatures aren't so high and the crowds are smaller.

Date Completed: _____

☐ **Swim in the Dead Sea.** Earth's lowest elevation on land. The deepest hypersaline lake in the world. With a salinity of 34.2%, it is one of the world's saltiest bodies of water which makes swimming in it similar to floating. This salinity makes for a harsh environment in which plants and animals cannot flourish, hence its name. October to April are the best times to visit.

Date Completed: _____

Turkey

☐ **Kayak in the Blue Lagoon.** This lagoon is the much-photographed gem of Turkey's Southern Coast, famous for its ever-varying shades of turquoise and azure with soft sands. Separated from the main beach by a sandbar and narrow channel, the lagoon beckons you into its shallow waters. You can immerse yourself, paddle barefoot along the shoreline or swim across to the tiny island at the mouth of the lagoon. No boats are allowed in to disrupt the peaceful atmosphere. Canoes and paddle-boats can be rented to explore the rocky shores of the inner lagoon and search for mussels, or you can snorkel to discover the myriad of tiny fish which start their life in these sheltered waters. The best time to visit for both the sun and lack of crowds is in the spring and autumn - May through June and September through October.

Date Completed: _____

☐ **Hot Air Balloon Festival in Göreme.** Just east of town is the Göreme Open Air Museum, with cave churches and frescoes from the 10th to 12th centuries. Southwest is Uçhisar Castle, a fortification carved into a large rock, with panoramic views from the top. To the north, the landscape at Paşabağ Valley is known for Cappadocia's "fairy chimneys," which are cone-shaped rock formations. They brought the festival back last year after a hiatus, but check for the best times to go. March through June and September through November are less crowded and not too cold.

Date Completed: _____

☐ **Get Scrubbed at a Hammam.** A gently heated, tiled room with a heated marble slab. Visitors lie on the stone slab and are exfoliated, then massaged with oils and finally washed clean with hot water.

Date Completed: _____

Place I Visited _____

About the Culture
_____
_____
_____
_____
_____

What I Learned
_____
_____
_____
_____
_____

My Reflection
_____
_____
_____
_____
_____

A Treasured Memory
_____
_____
_____
_____
_____

A Treasured Memory
_____
_____
_____
_____
_____

India

☐ **The Taj Mahal.** Meaning "The Crown of the Palace", it is an ivory-white marble mausoleum on the south bank of the Yamuna river in the Indian city of Agra. It was commissioned in 1632 by the Mughal emperor Shah Jahan to house the tomb of his favorite wife, Mumtaz Mahal; it also houses the tomb of Shah Jahan himself. The Best time to visit is in the winter months from November to February to avoid the heat and the summer rainy season.
Date Completed: _____

☐ **Elephant Festival and Holi (Festival of Colors).** Elephant Festival is celebrated in Jaipur city in Rajasthan state in India. It is held on the day of the Holi festival and features elephant polo and elephant dancing. The festival signifies the arrival of spring, the end of winter, the blossoming of love, and for many a festive day to meet others, play and laugh, forget and forgive, and repair broken relationships. It falls around the middle of March.
Date Completed: _____

☐ **Get a Henna tattoo.** Henna is a dye prepared from the plant Lawsonia inermis. Henna is referred to as temporary body art resulting from the staining of the skin from the dyes.
Date Completed: _____

Maldives

☐ **Sea of Stars.** A beautiful phenomenon which occurs during late summer months in the reefs of the Maldives, caused by bioluminescent phytoplankton called Lingulodinium polyedrum. The best time to visit is between May and November.
Date Completed: _____

United Arab Emirates

☐ **Ride a camel in Abu Dhabi.** You get to experience a dune bash and desert activities in comfort and safety capped by an evening at a traditional Bedouin camp. You can sand board, ride a camel, watch the sunset, enjoy a barbecue-buffet dinner and stargaze by the campfire.
Date Completed: _____

☐ **Ride the elevator to the top of Dubai's Burj Khalifa.** Venture up the world's tallest building.
Date Completed: _____

Place I Visited _____

About the Culture
_____
_____
_____
_____
_____

What I Learned
_____
_____
_____
_____
_____

My Reflection
_____
_____
_____
_____
_____

A Treasured Memory
_____
_____
_____
_____
_____

A Treasured Memory
_____
_____
_____
_____
_____

Cambodia

☐ **Angkor Wat.** This Hindu temple complex is the largest religious monument in the world. Originally constructed as a Hindu temple dedicated to the god Vishnu for the Khmer Empire, it was gradually transformed into a Buddhist temple towards the end of the 12th century. The best time to visit is during the dry season from late November to early April.

Date Completed: _____

Vietnam

☐ **The Hang Sơn Đoòng Cave.** The world's largest natural cave was just discovered in 1990! The best time to travel is from February to August. The remaining months are the rainy season, which is very dangerous for travelers. From February to April, the weather in Sơn Đoòng is very cool. It is perfect to discover the cave.

Date Completed: _____

☐ **Cycle Rice fields.** Mù Cang Chải is located at the foot of the Hoang Lien Son mountain range. To get to this place, you have to cross the Khau Phạ Pass, one of the most winding and dangerous passes in the country. But it's completely worth it: Mù Cang Chải has the most stunning rice terraces in Vietnam.

Date Completed: _____

Thailand

☐ **Songkran Festival.** The biggest water fight in the world, it celebrates the Thai New Year. I recommend attending it in Chiang Mai, but I may be biased. Anywhere is probably amazing. It is between April 13-15 every year.

Date Completed: _____

☐ **Volunteer at an elephant rescue.** They have a ton of these all over, but I am biased and love the one in Chiang Mai. This is a whole day filled with feeding, bathing and playing with rescued elephants.

Date Completed: _____

Place I Visited _____

About the Culture
_____
_____
_____
_____
_____

What I Learned
_____
_____
_____
_____
_____

My Reflection
_____
_____
_____
_____
_____

A Treasured Memory
_____
_____
_____
_____
_____

A Treasured Memory
_____
_____
_____
_____
_____

Japan

☐ **Shirakawa-gō.** These historic villages are one of Japan's UNESCO World Heritage Sites. These villages are well-known for their clusters of farmhouses, constructed in the architectural style known as gasshō-zukuri, which are designed to easily shed snow from their roofs. Spring is considered the best time to visit Japan, simply because you can enjoy the charming Cherry Blossoms collaborating with the historic Japanese village from mid-April to early May.
        Date Completed: _____

☐ **The Sapporo Snow Festival.** For one week every year, Sapporo hosts a giant festival of snow and ice. It is held for seven days sometime in the beginning of February, so look up the dates if you are going to go.
        Date Completed: _____

☐ **Kyoto.** Once the capital of Japan, it is famous for its numerous classical Buddhist temples, as well as gardens, imperial palaces, Shinto shrines and traditional wooden houses. It's also known for formal traditions such as kaiseki dining, consisting of multiple courses of precise dishes, and geisha, female entertainers often found in the Gion district. The best times to visit Kyoto are October/November and March/April/May, but you can go anytime as the weather is temperate.
        Date Completed: _____

☐ **Watch sumo wrestling.** Sumo is a form of competitive full-contact wrestling where a rikishi attempts to force his opponent out of a circular ring or into touching the ground with any body part other than the soles of his feet. The sport originated in Japan, the only country where it is practiced professionally.
        Date Completed: _____

☐ **Attend a Japanese tea ceremony.** It is a very important ritual that holds a lot of meaning within the culture. The tea ceremony represents purity, tranquility, respect and harmony and a lot of preparation goes into this important event.
        Date Completed: _____

☐ **Watch a geisha dance.** A woman highly trained in the arts of music, dance and entertaining. Geisha is Japanese for "person of art." She spends many years learning to play various musical instruments, sing, dance and be the perfect hostess in a party of men.
        Date Completed: _____

☐ **Senso-Ji Complex.** Make a beeline for the Senso-ji Temple, the city's premier Buddhist spot.
        Date Completed: _____

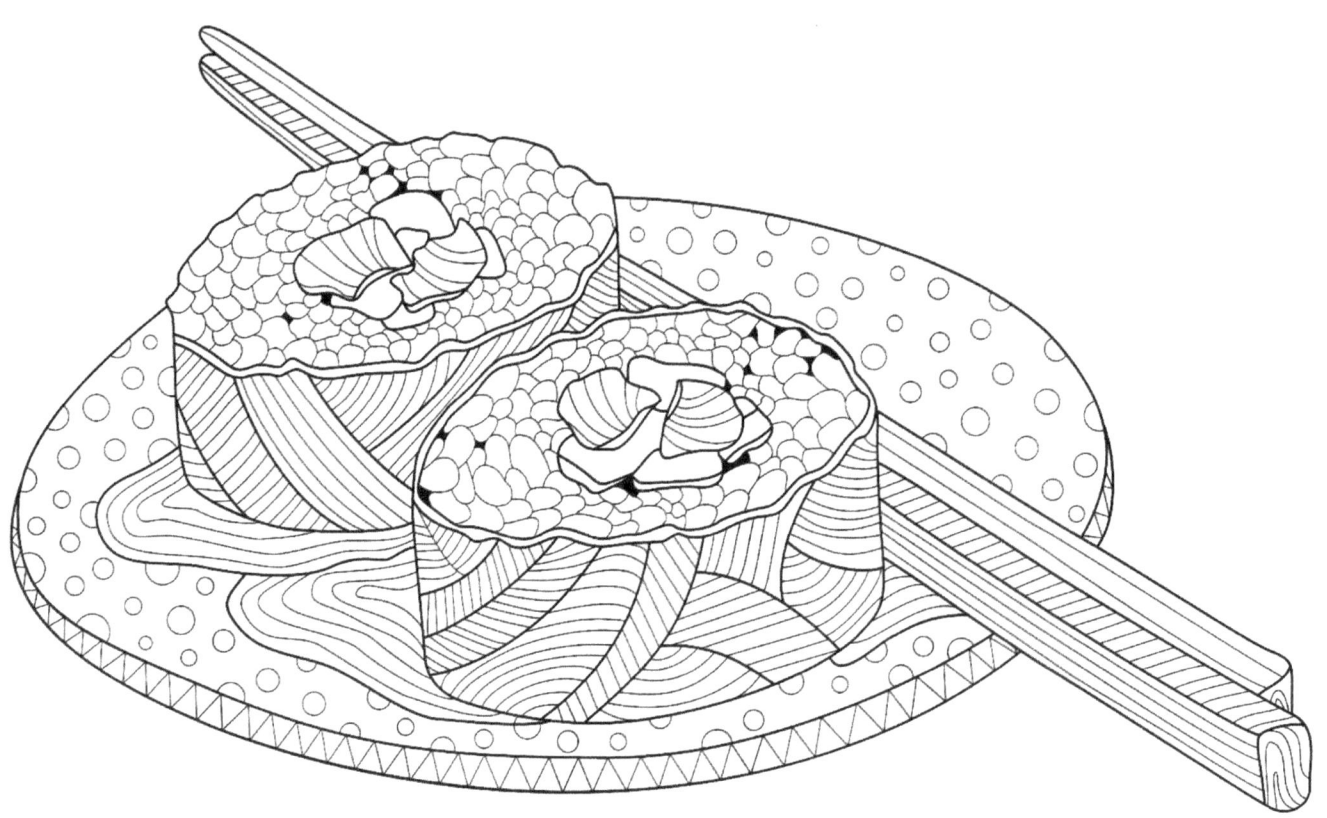

Place I Visited _____

About the Culture
_____
_____
_____
_____
_____

What I Learned
_____
_____
_____
_____
_____

My Reflection
_____
_____
_____
_____
_____

A Treasured Memory
_____
_____
_____
_____
_____

A Treasured Memory
_____
_____
_____
_____
_____

Myanmar

☐ **The Golden Rock.** Also known as Kyaiktiyo Pagoda, it is located in the Mon State of Burma. It is a popular Buddhist Pilgrimage site. Known as the Golden Rock, it is covered in gold leaves pasted on by devotees after the pilgrimage as a sign of respect to gain merit and purify their souls.

Date Completed: _____

Philippines

☐ **Canyoneering the Kawasan Falls.** This series of beautiful waterfalls with a mystical blue-turquoise color should most certainly be on your itinerary. Pretty much one of the most famous Instagram-worthy photo-ops out there. If you go early in the morning before nine, you'll have the best chance of beating the crowds. However, it does take 5-6 hours for the canyoneering, so keep that in mind.

Date Completed: _____

☐ **Boracay.** The island has become famous around the world for its beautiful white beaches. It is only 7km in length and at its narrowest just 500m wide, but people flock here for the outstanding beauty that the island offers.

Date Completed: _____

Singapore

☐ **Gardens by the bay.** The Gardens by the Bay is a nature park in the Central Region of Singapore, adjacent to the Marina Reservoir. The park consists of three waterfront gardens: Bay South Garden, Bay East Garden and Bay Central Garden. Its Flower Dome is the largest glass greenhouse in the world.

Date Completed: _____

☐ **Stay at the Marina Bay Sands.** Performances and cutting-edge art exhibitions are put on at the futuristic Esplanade Theatre. The neighborhood has a diverse range of eating options, from low-key food centers to upscale restaurants.

Date Completed: _____

Place I Visited _____

About the Culture
_____
_____
_____
_____
_____

What I Learned
_____
_____
_____
_____
_____

My Reflection
_____
_____
_____
_____
_____

A Treasured Memory
_____
_____
_____
_____
_____

A Treasured Memory
_____
_____
_____
_____
_____

Other Asia Countries

- ☐ Afghanistan
- ☐ Armenia
- ☐ Azerbaijan
- ☐ Bahrain
- ☐ Bangladesh
- ☐ Bhutan
- ☐ Brunel
- ☐ Cyprus
- ☐ Georgia
- ☐ Indonesia
- ☐ Iran
- ☐ Iraq
- ☐ Israel
- ☐ Kazakhstan
- ☐ Kuwait
- ☐ Kyrgyzstan
- ☐ Laos
- ☐ Lebanon
- ☐ Mongolia
- ☐ North Korea
- ☐ Oman
- ☐ Pakistan
- ☐ Palestine State
- ☐ Qatar
- ☐ Saudi Arabia
- ☐ South Korea
- ☐ Sri Lanka
- ☐ Syria
- ☐ Tajikistan
- ☐ Timor-Leste
- ☐ Turkmenistan
- ☐ Uzbekistan
- ☐ Yemen

Places I would like to go in Asia

A Treasured Memory in_____

_____
_____
_____
_____

A Treasured Memory in_____

_____
_____
_____
_____

A Treasured Memory in_____

_____
_____
_____
_____

A Treasured Memory in_____

_____
_____
_____
_____

A Treasured Memory in_____

_____
_____
_____
_____

A Treasured Memory in_____

_____
_____
_____
_____

OCEANIA

Australia

☐ **The Great Barrier Reef.** The Great Barrier Reef is the world's largest coral reef system composed of over 2,900 individual reefs and 900 islands. The best time to visit is between June through October, but be aware that is peak season. The best activity here is scuba diving.
Date Completed: _____

☐ **The Outback.** Its gateway is the isolated town of Alice Springs and its landmarks include Uluru, Australia's iconic red-rock monolith. You may also see a kangaroo or two. See if you can eat with them or if there is some type of tour. They are so cute.
Date Completed: _____

☐ **Sail the Whitsundays.** This cluster of 74 Islands lies between the northeast coast of Queensland, Australia, and the Great Barrier Reef. Most of the islands are uninhabited. They're characterized by dense rainforest, hiking trails and white sand beaches. The town of Airlie Beach on the mainland is the region's central hub.
Date Completed: _____

New Zealand

☐ **Kayak Milford Sound.** Known for towering Mitre Peak, plus rainforests and waterfalls like Stirling and Bowen falls, which plummet down its sheer sides. The fiord is home to fur seal colonies, penguins and dolphins. The Milford Discovery Centre and Underwater Observatory offers views of rare black coral and other marine life. Boat tours are a popular way to explore.
Date Completed: _____

☐ **Explore the Waitomo Glowworm Cave.** Thousands of glow-worms light up the Glowworm Caves. The vast Ruakuri Cave features waterfalls and limestone formations. West, Mangapohue Natural Bridge is a high limestone arch over Mangapohue Stream. Northeast of the village, Otorohanga Kiwi House shelters several species of the rare native kiwi bird.
Date Completed: _____

☐ **Kaikoura dolphin swim experience.** Just off the coast of the small South Island town is home to the Dusky Dolphin. This species is known for being small and very playful. They are quite the acrobats, and can often be seen doing back flips out of the water.
Date Completed: _____

Place I Visited _____

About the Culture
_____
_____
_____
_____
_____

What I Learned
_____
_____
_____
_____
_____

My Reflection
_____
_____
_____
_____
_____

A Treasured Memory
_____
_____
_____
_____
_____

A Treasured Memory
_____
_____
_____
_____
_____

Samoa

☐ **To Sua Ocean Trench in the Lotofoga village.** A scenic clear-water swimming hole with a diving board, plus landscaped gardens & picnic huts. There is no information on the best time to go, which I am guessing means it's not that populated! Bonus...You're welcome.
Date Completed: _____

Fiji

☐ **Fiji Mamanuca Islands.** The Mamanuca Islands of Fiji are a volcanic archipelago lying to the west of Nadi and to the south of the Yasawa Islands. A popular tourist destination, it consists of about 20 islands, but about seven of these are covered by the Pacific Ocean at high tide. The best time to visit Fiji is from late October to early November when the cost of getting and staying there has not yet reached its peak. During this period, the weather is dry, settled and warm and the beaches and resorts are far less crowded as school is still in session.
Date Completed: _____

☐ **The Yasawa Islands.** This chain of 20 islands garners attention for its lush landscapes, striking volcanic peaks, sparkling blue lagoons and ever-present sunshine.
Date Completed: _____

Palau

☐ **Swim with jelly fish in Lake Palau.** It is now re-opened to the public, so you can now swim among thousands of the beautiful sea creatures again.
Date Completed: _____

☐ **Get a natural mud bath in Palau's Milky Way.** A natural mud bath in the most brilliant blue waters of Palau, the Milky Way located in the rock islands of this Micronesian country, is known for its therapeutic properties. Locals claim that bathing in the white limestone mud found on the water's floor will make you look ten years younger.
Date Completed: _____

Place I Visited _____

About the Culture
_____
_____
_____
_____
_____
_____

What I Learned
_____
_____
_____
_____
_____
_____

My Reflection
_____
_____
_____
_____
_____
_____

A Treasured Memory
_____
_____
_____
_____
_____
_____

A Treasured Memory
_____
_____
_____
_____
_____
_____

Other Oceania Countries

☐ Kiribati

☐ Marshall Islands

☐ Micronesia

☐ Nauru

☐ New Zealand

☐ Papua New Guinea

☐ Solomon Islands

☐ Tonga

☐ Tuvalu

☐ Vanuatu

Places I would like to go in Oceania

A Treasured Memory in_____

_____
_____
_____
_____

A Treasured Memory in_____

_____
_____
_____
_____

A Treasured Memory in_____

_____
_____
_____
_____

A Treasured Memory in_____

_____
_____
_____
_____

A Treasured Memory in_____

_____
_____
_____
_____

A Treasured Memory in_____

_____
_____
_____
_____

Europe

Italy

☐ **Ride a gondola in Venice.** A traditional, flat-bottomed Venetian rowing boat, well suited to the conditions of the Venetian lagoon. During the day you will be in the direct sun most of the time so be careful. If you go during mid-February through early July, catch the Carnevale and wear a famous Venetian mask. According to Venetian tradition, Venice's Carnival got its start in 1162, when townspeople celebrated a victory over the Patriarch of Aquileia.
Date Completed: _____

☐ **The Roman Colosseum.** An oval amphitheater in the center of the city of Rome. Built of travertine limestone, tuff, and brick-faced concrete, it was the largest amphitheater ever constructed at the time and held up to 80,000 spectators. The best time of day to visit is right when it opens or 1-2 hours before closing, which changes throughout the year and is based on the sunset time. While you are there be sure to get some gelato too.
Date Completed: _____

☐ **Stomp grapes in a vineyard in Tuscany.** Ever since I was little and watched the rerun of "I Love Lucy" with her stomping grapes in a wood barrel, there is nothing I've wanted to do more. Grapes are ready to be harvested in Italy in early to mid-fall, most often during October. While in Tuscany you should also stay in a Villa, like in the movie *Under the Tuscan Sun*.
Date Completed: _____

☐ **The Sistine Chapel.** The Sistine Chapel is a chapel in the Apostolic Palace, the official residence of the pope, in Vatican City and the classic work of art by Michelangelo.
Date Completed: _____

☐ **Burano.** Known for its brightly colored fishermen's houses and its casual eateries serving seafood from the lagoon, it's just a boat ride away from Venice and well-worth the day trip.
Date Completed: _____

☐ **Watch an opera at the world-famous Teatro alla Scala.** If you are visiting it just to see the building and the museum, the best time to go is during the spring or fall. During these periods of time, it is a little bit less crowded than the other parts of the year.
Date Completed: _____

☐ **Make a wish in the Trevi Fountain.** The most famous fountain in the world.
Date Completed: _____

☐ **Mysteries of Pompeii.** The preserved site features excavated ruins of streets and houses that visitors can freely explore.
Date Completed: _____

☐ **Examine Michelangelo's David.** Despite the omnipresence of Michelangelo's iconic sculpture, David deserves to be inspected up close. He is breathtaking: an almost 17-foot-tall marvel in marble who is alternately human and divine. David commands your attention from all vantage points. Your perspective changes as you look left at the muscle definition Michelangelo managed to convey in hunks of stone, and then look right, into the frightened but determined eyes of a simple man about to face off against the giant Goliath.
          Date Completed: _____

☐ **Climb to the top of St. Peter's Basilica.** One of Italy's most spectacular churches. While the interiors are world-famous, don't skimp on heading outside the church for some views either.
          Date Completed: _____

☐ **Drive the Amalfi Coast.** Known for its dramatic bluffs, pastel-hued villages, and cliff-hugging roads, the Amalfi Coast is arguably Italy's most scenic stretch of coastline.
          Date Completed: _____

☐ **La Traviata, the original opera with ballet.** Ballet began in the Italian Renaissance courts and spread from Italy to France by Catherine de' Medici. Later it developed into a concert dance form in France and Russia. King Louis XIV founded the Académie Royale de Musique from which the Paris Opera Ballet developed as the first professional ballet company.
          Date Completed: _____

☐ **Tour Lake Como by boat.** The most beautiful lake in Italy's Lake District, Como is surrounded by steep mountain slopes covered in lush greenery and dotted with compact towns and magnificent villas.
          Date Completed: _____

☐ **Take a boat trip to the Blue Grotto.** One of the premium sights in Capri is the Blue Grotto, also known as the Grotta Azzurra. The grotto is the result of a cavern which is filled with water that glows a luminescent blue when the sun hits it through shafts in the sides of the rock.
          Date Completed: _____

☐ **The Leaning Tower of Pisa.** A fluke of architecture, when the tower was constructed it immediately started to sink into the marshy ground beneath it. This gave the tower its signature crooked stance, and at various times in its existence it has been both open and closed to the public as architects struggle to asses if it is safe to enter.
          Date Completed: _____

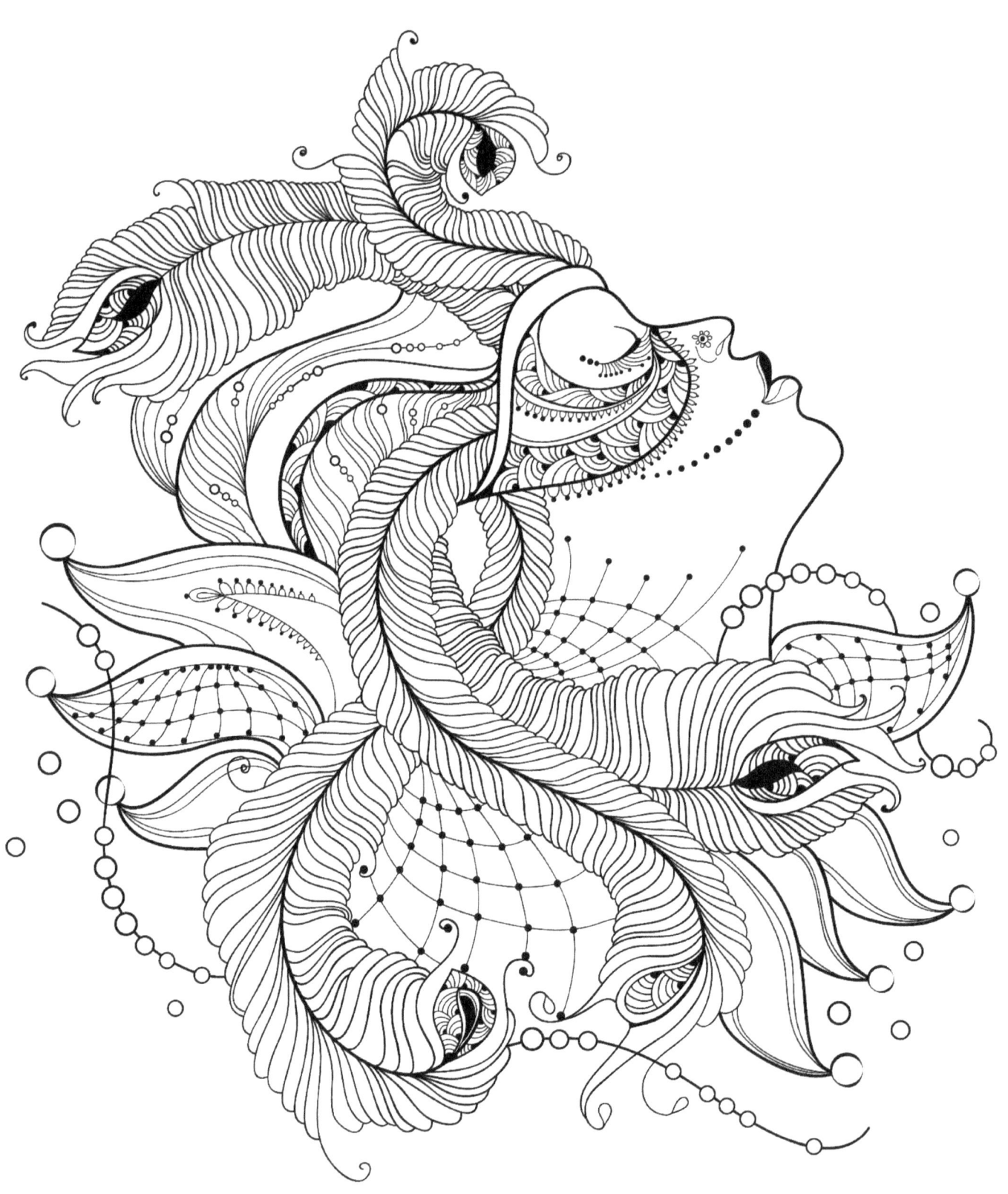

Place I Visited _____

About the Culture
_____
_____
_____
_____
_____

What I Learned
_____
_____
_____
_____
_____

My Reflection
_____
_____
_____
_____
_____

A Treasured Memory
_____
_____
_____
_____
_____

A Treasured Memory
_____
_____
_____
_____
_____

Germany

☐ **Oktoberfest.** It begins on the second to last Saturday in September at noon when the mayor of Munich taps the first barrel at the Schottenhamel Tent, crying "O'zapft is" (It's open).
Date Completed: _____

☐ **Rothenberg.** A romantic medieval town with stunning architecture. September and October can be excellent months to visit, as the light is still good but the crowds will have mostly gone.
Date Completed: _____

☐ **Walk the Berlin Wall.** The 13-mile-long structure is now converted to a series of paved pathways, divided into 14 stages that pass from rural idyll to the bustling city center. Along the way, you'll spot abandoned watchtowers and stretches covered in colorful murals.
Date Completed: _____

Netherlands

☐ **Smoke Weed in Amsterdam and go to the Van Gogh Museum.** Trust me on this one, you will spend hours looking at the vivid brush strokes of the famous Vincent and maybe even feel like you're morphing into the painting itself. Avoid the peak season which is July and August in the Dutch capital. The best time to visit the city is late spring or early fall.
Date Completed: _____

☐ **Zaanse Schans.** The sights include a shipyard, a grocery store, a pewter factory, and a range of dainty green wooden houses. You will also find some graceful windmills, although out of the 600 that would have dotted the area in the days of old, only five now remain and can be visited by the public. You will also find other fun activities like a clog making demonstration.
Date Completed: _____

Denmark

☐ **Gasadalur, Faroe Islands.** This magical village looks out onto the grey sea from atop a beautiful hidden waterfall. Other mystified places to visit is the Múlafossur waterfall, Tindhólmur Island, and some light hiking in Drangarnir and Arnafjall. The best time to visit is from June until October, when it will be very cold, but with limited rainfall.
Date Completed: _____

Place I Visited _____

About the Culture

_____
_____
_____
_____
_____

What I Learned

_____
_____
_____
_____
_____

My Reflection

_____
_____
_____
_____
_____

A Treasured Memory

_____
_____
_____
_____
_____

A Treasured Memory

_____
_____
_____
_____
_____

Greece

☐ **The Parthenon.** A former temple on the Athenian Acropolis, it is dedicated to the goddess Athena. The best time to visit is during the summer after 5pm. The brilliant light of the late-afternoon hours will only enhance your experience.
Date Completed: _____

☐ **Go Island Hopping.** The most well-known islands of Santorini and Mykonos are a must, but find the smaller islands that aren't so popular but still enchantingly beautiful so you aren't overwhelmed by tourists. There are estimates of 12,000 to 6,000 islands in Greece! You are bound to find one uninhabited.
Date Completed: _____

☐ **Mount Olympus.** Known in Greek mythology as the spot where Zeus sat on his throne, as well as where Hades ruled the Underworld, as you climb it you can imagine the legends that are associated with this mountain.
Date Completed: _____

☐ **Delphi.** It sits on the sides of Mount Parnassus and was a popular pilgrimage spot in the days of old for people to pay homage to Apollo, the ancient Greek god of healing, music, light, and prophecy.
Date Completed: _____

☐ **The Corinth Canal.** Construction for it began under Nero the ancient Roman emperor, and took centuries to build before finally being completed by the French as late as the 19th century. One of the other main attractions on the canal is the Zulu Bungee Jump, which is certainly not for those who don't have a head for heights, but is also an amazing way to take in all the majesty of the canal.
Date Completed: _____

Croatia

☐ **Yacht Week.** This is what I want to do for my bachelorette party. Sailing around the islands and partying every night. You and your girlfriends get your own yacht! This just sounds like the best thing ever.
Date Completed: _____

☐ **Listen to the sea organ in Zadar.** Created by local architect Nikola Bašić, the Sea Organ is a unique musical experience where relaxing melodies are created from the wind and the ebb and flow of the sea.
Date Completed: _____

Place I Visited _____

About the Culture
_____
_____
_____
_____
_____

What I Learned
_____
_____
_____
_____
_____

My Reflection
_____
_____
_____
_____
_____

A Treasured Memory
_____
_____
_____
_____
_____

A Treasured Memory
_____
_____
_____
_____
_____

United Kingdom

☐ **Meet the Queen of England.** Or at least go to Buckingham Palace if you can't find her. The best time to visit London is March through May when the temperatures are mild and the city's parks are green and blooming.

Date Completed: _____

☐ **Stonehenge.** Stonehenge is a prehistoric monument in Wiltshire, England. It consists of a ring of standing stones, each around thirteen feet high, seven feet wide. The best time of day to visit Stonehenge is before 9:30am or after 4pm during the summer, and after 2pm in the winter.
Date Completed: _____

☐ **Glastonbury Abbey.** Glastonbury is a town in southwest England. It's known for its ancient and medieval sites, many rich in myth. Glastonbury Tor is a tower-topped hill linked to Arthurian legend, overlooking the marshy Somerset Levels. Once said to be King Arthur's burial place, Glastonbury Abbey is a ruined monastery dating to the 7th century.
Date Completed: _____

❖ **Other things to do in England:**

☐ See the changing of the guard.

☐ Attend a proper British afternoon tea.

☐ Relish cheap seats at Shakespeare's Globe Theatre.

☐ Black pool illuminations.

☐ **Sleep in a castle in Scotland.** I don't know why this sounds so appealing, but pretending to be a royal in the 1500s is my jam. There are two I have found that look magical, the Glenapp and the Inverlochy. It's best to visit during the spring and autumn months.
Date Completed: _____

❖ **Other things to do in Scotland:**

☐ Fingal's Cave on the island of Staffa.

☐ "Up Helly Aa" Fire festival in Shetland.

☐ Search for Nessie at Loch Ness

Place I Visited _____

About the Culture
_____
_____
_____
_____
_____

What I Learned
_____
_____
_____
_____
_____

My Reflection
_____
_____
_____
_____
_____

A Treasured Memory
_____
_____
_____
_____
_____

A Treasured Memory
_____
_____
_____
_____
_____

France

☐ **The Eiffel Tower.** A wrought-iron lattice tower on the Champ de Mars in Paris, France. It is named after the engineer Gustave Eiffel, whose company designed and built the tower. I recommend staying at a hotel nearby, so you can drink wine and enjoy the tower's nightly light shows while Facetiming your friends back home. The best time to visit Paris is from April to June and October to early November, when the weather is mild and enjoyable and the tourist crowds are smaller than during the summer.
Date Completed: _____

☐ **The Louvre.** The world's largest art museum and a historic monument in Paris, France. It houses some of the greatest works of art such as the Mona Lisa and the Winged Victory.
Date Completed: _____

☐ **Mont St. Michael.** A magical island topped by a gravity-defying medieval monastery; the Mont-Saint-Michel counts among France's most stunning sights. The best time to visit Mont Saint-Michel is March to October when the weather is at its best. July and August are high season so crowds are at their thickest.
Date Completed: _____

☐ **Sunbathe topless in the French Riviera.** I feel you have to try it at least once. Remember to find out the sunbathing regulations in the area, however, to make sure it is allowed where you are.
Date Completed: _____

☐ **Sleep in an overwater bungalow in Bora Bora.** Even though this is super expensive, and probably better with a significant other, I still put it on the list.
Date Completed: _____

Switzerland

☐ **Ski the Swiss Alps in Zermatt.** At an elevation of around 1,600m, the town lies below the iconic, pyramid-shaped Matterhorn peak. Late February to mid-March is when the crowds start to clear out.
Date Completed: _____

☐ **Eat traditional fondue.** Popularized as a Swiss national dish by the Swiss Cheese Union (Schweizerische Käseunion) in the 1930s as a way of increasing cheese consumption.
Date Completed: _____

Place I Visited _____

About the Culture
_____
_____
_____
_____
_____

What I Learned
_____
_____
_____
_____
_____

My Reflection
_____
_____
_____
_____
_____

A Treasured Memory
_____
_____
_____
_____
_____

A Treasured Memory
_____
_____
_____
_____
_____

Ukraine

☐ **Tunnel of love in Klevan.** The Tunnel of Love is a section of industrial railway located near Klevan, Ukraine, that links it with Orzhiv. It is a railway surrounded by green arches and is about 2-3 miles long. The best time to visit is the end of spring and early summer. During this time, the greenery still looks fresh and not too dry or yellowish as it can tend to get by the end of the summer.

Date Completed: _____

Russia

☐ **White Knights Festival in St. Petersburg.** An annual summer festival in Saint Petersburg celebrating its near-midnight sun phenomena due to its location near the Arctic Circle. Each year around April 21 through August 21, the skies only reach twilight and never become fully dark.

Date Completed: _____

☐ **Red Square, Moscow.** Red Square is a city square in Moscow. It separates the Kremlin, the former royal citadel and now the official residence of the President of Russia, from a historic merchant quarter known as Kitay-gorod.

Date Completed: _____

Romania

☐ **Visit Dracula's Castle in Transylvania.** Bram Stoker never visited Romania. He depicted the fictional Dracula's castle based upon a description of Bran Castle that was available to him in turn-of-the-century Britain. Indeed, the depiction of the castle from the etching in the first edition of "Dracula" is strikingly similar to Bran Castle, and no other in all of Romania.

Date Completed: _____

☐ **Bigar Cascade Falls.** This place is so lovely, it is even called "the miracle from the Minis Canyon" by the locals. The rounded waterfall is almost eight meters high, and falls over an unusual and dramatic green carpet of moss. Unlike more roaring falls, this waterwork flows over the apex of a fat, rounded stone, and is diverted into a sheet of countless small streams that issue from the bottom of the stone, which juts out over the basin below.

Date Completed: _____

Place I Visited _____

About the Culture

_____
_____
_____
_____
_____

What I Learned

_____
_____
_____
_____
_____

My Reflection

_____
_____
_____
_____
_____

A Treasured Memory

_____
_____
_____
_____
_____

A Treasured Memory

_____
_____
_____
_____
_____

Portugal

☐ **Umbrella Street.** In select areas of the city of Águeda, Portugal, you will find streets lined with colorful umbrellas. The installation, known as the Umbrella Sky Project, is part of the local AgitÁgueda Art Festival. It takes place every year between July and September. The best time to visit is July, when you not only get to see the Umbrella Sky Project but also the rest of the AgitÁgueda Festival.
Date Completed: _____

☐ **Bell-Mouth Spillway.** At first glance, you might see this manmade hole in the Conchos Dam which allows water to flow down into it, and mistake it for a vortex into another dimension. It is actually a method for controlling the release of water from the dam and diverting it elsewhere.
Date Completed: _____

☐ **Stand on the end of the continent.** Sagres is a wind-swept outpost set on a thin peninsula at the far southeastern edge of Portugal, AKA the very edge of Europe.
Date Completed: _____

Spain

☐ **La Tomatina Bunol.** A festival that is held in the Valencian town of Buñol, in which participants get involved in a tomato fight purely for entertainment purposes. It usually happens during the last days of August.
Date Completed: _____

☐ **Girona.** It's known for its medieval architecture, walled Old Quarter (Barri Vell) and the Roman remains of the Força Vella fortress. Landscaped gardens line the Passeig Arqueològic, a walkway following the Old Quarter's medieval walls, which include watchtowers with sweeping views.
Date Completed: _____

❖ **Other things to do in Spain:**

☐ **See a Flamenco show.**

☐ **Watch a Bull Fight.**

☐ **Marvel at Gaudi's Sagrada Familia Church.**

Place I Visited _____

About the Culture
_____
_____
_____
_____
_____

What I Learned
_____
_____
_____
_____
_____

My Reflection
_____
_____
_____
_____
_____

A Treasured Memory
_____
_____
_____
_____
_____

A Treasured Memory
_____
_____
_____
_____
_____

Iceland

☐ **The actual Blue Lagoon.** A Blue Lagoon is a place where the powers of geothermal seawater create transformational spa journeys. Winter months are typically the calmest, particularly in December and January, outside of the holiday period.

Date Completed: _____

☐ **Check out the animals on Puffin Island.** The islands of Akureyri and Lundey are known for their gorgeous and cuddly puffin colonies. You can see a plethora of other wildlife including cormorants, ducks, seagulls, and guillemots. The island is uninhabited but you can take a boat across from the mainland and watch the puffins nesting and tending to their young.

Date Completed: _____

Norway

☐ **Float down the Geirangerfjord.** The deep blue UNESCO-protected Geirangerfjord river is surrounded by majestic, snow-covered mountain peaks, wild waterfalls and lush, green vegetation.

Date Completed: _____

☐ **Marvel at the fjords of Western Norway.** You can't think of Norway without thinking of fjords, and the western part of the country features two of the country's most spectacular examples: Geirangerfjord and Nærøyfjord. These UNESCO-listed wonders are bookended by steep crystalline rock walls and rugged mountains, and feature landscapes dotted with waterfalls, glacial lakes, and forests.

Date Completed: _____

Ireland

☐ **Celebrate St. Patrick's Day in Dublin.** Make sure you book early and arrive even earlier to the festivities. And, obviously, don't get caught without wearing green.

Date Completed: _____

☐ **Geek out at Trinity College.** Aside from having a beautiful campus, Trinity College houses the famous Book of Kells, a 9th-century manuscript penned by monks in amazingly intricate fonts and illustrations. When you're done perusing, a visit to the library's Long Room is an absolute must. You'll feel like you stepped directly into a Disney movie.

Date Completed: _____

Place I Visited _____

About the Culture

_____
_____
_____
_____
_____

What I Learned

_____
_____
_____
_____
_____

My Reflection

_____
_____
_____
_____
_____

A Treasured Memory

_____
_____
_____
_____
_____

A Treasured Memory

_____
_____
_____
_____
_____

Sweden

☐ **See the Northern Lights from the Ice Hotel in Sweden.** The Aurora Borealis appears during the beginning of September. By the time winter has fully set in around January, the Northern lights can be seen throughout Swedish Lapland. The last glimpses of these undulating rainbows can be caught as late as the end of March or even early April. The most spectacular displays usually take place around 10:00-11:00pm.

Date Completed: _____

☐ **Gamla Stan.** A small concentrated area where the city began in the middle of the 13th century. Much of the medieval enclave remains, although in typical Scandinavian style, it is freshly brushed and painted. Its charm is in the architecture along its narrow stone-paved lanes and around its squares, especially the main one, Stortorget, surrounded by old merchants' houses.

Date Completed: _____

Finland

☐ **Finnish Sauna.** There is nothing more Finnish than a sauna, and many Finns think you cannot grasp Finland or its culture without bathing in one.

Date Completed: _____

☐ **Sleep in a glass igloo.** The bright snow, the moon and the stars, and, if you are lucky, the Northern Lights, create magical surroundings.

Date Completed: _____

Poland

☐ **Take a carriage ride through Krakow's Old Town.** A picture-perfect city steeped in history and culture. The beautiful Old Town and medieval Wawel Palace are worth your time, especially if you take a ride in one of the city's famous horse-drawn carriages.

Date Completed: _____

☐ **Auschwitz.** The single most emotional and sobering reminder of the horrors of the Nazi regime in Europe. With exhibits that chronicle its transformation into to a death camp and the atrocities performed upon the minorities within, it's become not only a museum but a memorial to the Holocaust and the destruction of the European Jews. It's something that you should not miss experiencing.

Date Completed: _____

Place I Visited _____

About the Culture

_____
_____
_____
_____
_____

What I Learned

_____
_____
_____
_____
_____

My Reflection

_____
_____
_____
_____
_____

A Treasured Memory

_____
_____
_____
_____
_____

A Treasured Memory

_____
_____
_____
_____
_____

Other European Countries

- ☐ Albania
- ☐ Andorra
- ☐ Austria
- ☐ Belarus
- ☐ Belgium
- ☐ Bosnia and Herzegovina
- ☐ Bulgaria
- ☐ Czechia (Czech Republic)
- ☐ Estonia
- ☐ Holy See
- ☐ Hungary
- ☐ Latvia
- ☐ Liechtenstein
- ☐ Lithuania
- ☐ Luxembourg
- ☐ Malta
- ☐ Moldova
- ☐ Monaco
- ☐ Montenegro
- ☐ North Macedonia
- ☐ San Marino
- ☐ Serbia
- ☐ Slovakia
- ☐ Slovenia

Places I would like to go in Europe

A Treasured Memory in_____
_____
_____
_____
_____

A Treasured Memory in_____
_____
_____
_____
_____

A Treasured Memory in_____
_____
_____
_____
_____

A Treasured Memory in_____
_____
_____
_____
_____

A Treasured Memory in_____
_____
_____
_____
_____

A Treasured Memory in_____
_____
_____
_____
_____

NORTH AMERICA

United States of America

☐ **Dog Sledding in Alaska.** Dog sledding has been a popular sport in Alaska for generations. Iditarod mushers will take you on a dog sled ride, tell you stories from the world-famous race, and let you cuddle with sled dogs. It is usually offered year-round, so research when the best time would be for you to go.
Date Completed: _____

☐ **Haiku Stairs of Oahu, Hawaii.** Also known as the Stairway to Heaven. Right now, you can't climb them but you can see breathtaking views on the hike. The best months to visit Oahu are April, May, September, and October for great weather, fewer crowds, and fair rates.
Date Completed: _____

❖ **Other places to see in Hawaii:**

☐ Volcanoes.
☐ Turtle Bay.
☐ Shrimp trucks.

☐ **The Hollywood Sign in Los Angeles, California.** It's more than just nine white letters spelling out a city's name; it's one of the world's most evocative symbols – a universal metaphor for ambition, success and glamour. The best time of the year to hike to the Hollywood Sign is late-January to early-February or October through November when the views are the best. The temperatures are also on your side during these months.
Date Completed: _____

❖ **Other places to see in Los Angeles:**
☐ Shop on Rodeo Drive.
☐ Ride the Ferris wheel at the Santa Monica Pier.
☐ Hollywood Walk of Fame.
☐ Warner Brothers Studio Tour.

☐ **Golden Gate Bridge, San Francisco.** The Golden Gate Bridge is a suspension bridge spanning the Golden Gate, a one-mile-wide strait connecting San Francisco Bay and the Pacific Ocean. The best time to visit is between September and November.
Date Completed: _____

- ❖ **Other places to see in San Francisco:**
  - ☐ Alcatraz Island.
  - ☐ Ride a cable car.

☐ **Drive Route 66.** Historic Route 66 spans over 2,400 miles and crosses 8 states, starting in Chicago, Illinois and terminating at the Pacific Coast in Santa Monica, California.
Date Completed: _____

☐ **Burning Man in Nevada.** Contrary to popular belief, Burning Man is not a festival! It is a "city" that is constructed and inhabited for nine days every year around late August through early September in the Nevada desert. Almost everything at Burning Man, including the structures, decorations, commerce and festivities is created entirely by its citizens, who are active participants in the experience.
Date Completed: _____

☐ **Gamble in Las Vegas, Nevada.** Known as Block 16 and Block 17 in the beginning of the city's construction, Las Vegas boomed during the early days of gambling and liquor sales. Both blocks are where the nickname "Sin City" originated. The best time to visit is from March to May and from September to November. While you'll find plenty of travel deals throughout the year, the spring and fall shoulder seasons offer the most moderate weather.
Date Completed: _____

- ❖ **Other places to see in Las Vegas:**
  - ☐ Cirque Du Soleil performance.
  - ☐ Go to a hotel pool party.

☐ **Visit the Grand Canyon in Arizona.** With layered bands of red rock revealing millions of years of geological history, it is definitely a site to see if you go to Arizona. Best times to visit are March through May and September through November, when daytime temperatures are cool and the crowds are thin.
Date Completed: _____

- ❖ **Other places to visit in Arizona:**
  - ☐ Paria Canyon-Vermilion Cliffs.
  - ☐ Antelope Canyon.

☐ **Devil's Tower, Wyoming.** Devils Tower is a butte made of igneous rock in the Bear Lodge Ranger District of the Black Hills. The most popular time to visit is June through August. It's prime time for river rafting, hiking, mountain biking, wildlife viewing, and other outdoor activities.
Date Completed: _____

❖ **Other places to do in Wyoming:**
- ☐ Go camping.
- ☐ Yellowstone National Park.

☐ **White Water rafting in Middle Fork Salmon River in Idaho.** Late June to early August is the best time to go. The river has slowed, but the whitewater rapids are still challenging.
Date Completed: _____

☐ **Mount Rushmore in South Dakota.** A massive sculpture carved into the side of the mountain that was completed in 1941 under the direction of Gutzon Borglum. The sculpture's roughly 60-ft.-high granite faces depict U.S. presidents George Washington, Thomas Jefferson, Theodore Roosevelt and Abraham Lincoln.
Date Completed: _____

☐ **Mardi Gras in New Orleans.** Also known as Fat Tuesday, the carnival celebration begins on or after the Christian feasts of the Epiphany in January and culminates on the day before Ash Wednesday.
Date Completed: _____

☐ **Washington, D.C.** A compact city and the US capital bordering the states of Maryland and Virginia. It is defined by imposing neoclassical monuments and buildings – including the iconic ones that house the federal government's three branches. It's also home to iconic museums and performing arts venues. The best times to visit are from September to November and March to May.
Date Completed: _____

☐ **Go to the Kentucky Derby wearing a ridiculously amazing hat.** This horse race is held annually in Louisville, Kentucky, on the first Saturday in May, capping the two-week-long Kentucky Derby Festival.
Date Completed: _____

☐ **The Statue of Liberty in New York City.** "The Statue of Liberty Enlightening the World" was a gift of friendship from France to the United States and is recognized as a universal symbol of freedom and democracy. Fall is the most popular time to see New York city, but flow to the Statue of Liberty is quite moderate during this time. If visiting in summer, remember that June is the best month, with fewer crowds and nicer weather.
Date Completed: _____

❖ **Other places to see in New York:**
- ☐ Spend New Year's Eve in Time's Square.
- ☐ Go ice skating in Rockefeller plaza.

☐ See Niagara Falls.

☐ Spend Summer in the Hamptons.

☐ Attend a Broadway show.

☐ **Art Basel in Miami, Florida.** This ranks as the premier art show of the Americas, offering a platform for renowned artists and galleries. It occurs during late-June.
Date Completed: _____

☐ **Walt Disney World, Florida.** Enjoy bringing out your inner kid again. I would like to meet Prince Charming at the most magical-est place on earth.
Date Completed: _____

☐ **Drive across America from coast to coast.** I have done this twice; I feel like it would have been more fun if we had taken our time and stopped at more places. So, if you are going to do it, don't rush through it.
Date Completed: _____

☐ **Go to Walden Pond in Massachusetts and read Thoreau while drifting in a canoe.** Walden Pond is a lake in Concord, Massachusetts. A famous example of a kettle hole, it was formed by retreating glaciers 10,000–12,000 years ago. Again, this would probably be an amazingly romantic first date-type thing. But even if you are single, you can take in the beautiful scenery and read one of the best poets of our time.
Date Completed: _____

☐ **Party at a honky-tonk bar in Nashville, Tennessee.**
Date Completed: _____

☐ **Experience the foliage in New England.** And eat lobster rolls from a seaside shack in Maine.
Date Completed: _____

Place I Visited _____

About the Culture
_____
_____
_____
_____
_____

What I Learned
_____
_____
_____
_____
_____

My Reflection
_____
_____
_____
_____
_____

A Treasured Memory
_____
_____
_____
_____
_____

A Treasured Memory
_____
_____
_____
_____
_____

Canada

☐ **Moraine Lake, Alberta.** The most photographed lake in the world, enough said. The best time to go is from mid-June through the end of July. The melting glaciers and rising levels of the lake tend to crest around the middle of June. The full lake creates a distinct shade of blue as refraction from the rock floor colors the water.

Date Completed: _____

☐ **Bed down in an Igloo in Quebec.** There is a cool hotel that you need to experience here and it is Hôtel de Glace. Google this stuff! Maybe you do it when you have a boyfriend because it looks super romantic.

Date Completed: _____

☐ **Queen Charlotte Islands/Haida Gwaii, British Columbia.** Centuries-old totem poles stand in the remains of the Haida Nation village known as SGang Gwaay Llanagaay.

Date Completed: _____

☐ **Western Brook Pond, Newfoundland.** There are some places so breathtaking in Canada that even the best photographs barely convey the beauty and scale of them. Newfoundland's iconic Western Brook Pond Fjord located in Gros Morne National Park is one of those places. The best time to go is late May or mid-October. The best time of day for pictures is between 12:30 and 1:00pm. Even if you go in peak season around July and August, it is still not extremely crowded.

Date Completed: _____

☐ **Cavendish Beach, Prince Edward Island.** Home of one of the most beautiful beaches on the island that every single girl must experience. The sea is a cornucopia of culinary adventures for food-lovers. Feast on fresh lobster, oysters, PEI mussels and more, served up Island-style. The best time to go is between mid-July to mid-August.

Date Completed: _____

☐ **Abraham Lake, Alberta.** Large white bubbles are created in lakes and ponds when water-dwelling bacteria feed on decaying organic matter and expel methane gas. When the water freezes, the bubbles are suspended in the ice. The bubbles are so prominent under the frozen surface of Alberta's artificially created Abraham Lake, they lure visitors outdoors during wintry months.

Date Completed: _____

Place I Visited _____

About the Culture
_____
_____
_____
_____
_____

What I Learned
_____
_____
_____
_____
_____

My Reflection
_____
_____
_____
_____
_____

A Treasured Memory
_____
_____
_____
_____
_____

A Treasured Memory
_____
_____
_____
_____
_____

British Overseas Territory

☐ **Anguilla, Shoal Bay Village.** Located on the western end of Anguilla, Meads Bay is beloved for its silky-smooth sand, aquamarine waters and gorgeous views. The busiest month for tourism is January, followed by July and August. Prices for hotels and flights will be most expensive during these months, though you can save if you purchase well in advance. Tourists are unlikely to visit Shoal Bay in October.
Date Completed: _____

☐ **Turks and Caicos.** With its beautiful turquoise waters, white sand beaches and tropical climate, no wonder it's becoming the number one island. They even have their own ambassador dolphins, whatever that means, but DOLPHINS! The best time to go is April and May where that seems to be the sweet spot with fewer crowds and lower prices.
Date Completed: _____

Caribbean Islands

☐ **The Great Blue Hole in Belize.** A giant marine sinkhole off the coast of Belize. It lies near the center of Lighthouse Reef. Diving in Belize is possible year-round but the best time is between April and June. This is also the time when the whale sharks can be spotted. These months also see bigger crowds of divers at the Great Blue Hole. The wet season runs from June to November, but showers are quite short and bearable.
Date Completed: _____

☐ **Pig Island, Bahamas.** An uninhabited island located in Exuma, Bahamas. The island takes its unofficial name from the fact that it is populated by a colony of feral pigs that live on the island and in the surrounding shallows. Peak season is during the months of December to Mid-April. When a dangerous storm is brewing, the pigs are usually taken to shelter by a local water sports company. Most tours will start in the mornings between 8 am and 9 am, and again at sunset.
Date Completed: _____

Place I Visited _____

About the Culture
_____
_____
_____
_____
_____

What I Learned
_____
_____
_____
_____
_____

My Reflection
_____
_____
_____
_____
_____

A Treasured Memory
_____
_____
_____
_____
_____

A Treasured Memory
_____
_____
_____
_____
_____

Mexico

☐ **Chichén Itzá.** A massive step pyramid, known as El Castillo or Temple of Kukulcán, it dominates the ancient city, which thrived from around 600 A.D. to the 1200s. It is also one of the New Seven Wonders of the World. Graphic stone carvings survive at structures like the ball court, Temple of the Warriors and the Wall of the Skulls. Nightly sound-and-light shows illuminate the buildings' sophisticated geometry. Weather-wise, November through March is the best time to go, but this also brings the most crowds. For daily planning, it's best to arrive when they open, and avoid Sundays.
Date Completed: _____

☐ **Spring Break in Cabo San Lucas, Cancun, or Puerto Vallarta.** This is an absolute must wherever you decide to go. Mexico's beach cities are the staple spring break spots.
Date Completed: _____

☐ **Day of the Dead, Mexico City.** Developed from ancient traditions among its pre-Columbian cultures, it takes place on November 1st and 2nd.
Date Completed: _____

☐ **Tulum.** With white sands and beautifully clear waters, top-notch restaurants and beach clubs, and activities that range from swimming in stunning cenotes to visiting preserved Mayan ruins, it's clear to see why Tulum ends up on so many bucket lists. The best time to visit is between October and December.
Date Completed: _____

☐ **Ixtapa and Zihuatanejo.** These are two of the smaller beach towns and mostly unknown but still beautiful none the less. Best time to go is between December and April.
Date Completed: _____

❖ **Other Places to Visit in Mexico**
- ☐ **Grutas Tolantongo.**
- ☐ **Hierve el Aqua.**
- ☐ **Suytun Cenote.**
- ☐ **Edward James Surrealist Garden "Las Pozas".**
- ☐ **Cenote Tak Bi Ha.**
- ☐ **Tamasopo.**
- ☐ **Play Balandra in La Paz.**

Place I Visited _____

About the Culture
_____
_____
_____
_____
_____

What I Learned
_____
_____
_____
_____
_____
_____

My Reflection
_____
_____
_____
_____
_____
_____

A Treasured Memory
_____
_____
_____
_____
_____
_____

A Treasured Memory
_____
_____
_____
_____
_____
_____

Other North American Countries

- ☐ Antigua and Barbuda
- ☐ Barbados
- ☐ Costa Rica
- ☐ Cuba
- ☐ Dominica
- ☐ Dominican Republic
- ☐ El Salvador
- ☐ Grenada
- ☐ Guatemala
- ☐ Haiti
- ☐ Honduras
- ☐ Jamaica
- ☐ Nicaragua
- ☐ Panama
- ☐ Saint Kitts and Nevis
- ☐ Saint Lucia
- ☐ Saint Vincent and the Grenadines
- ☐ Trinidad and Tobago

Places I would like to go in North America

A Treasured Memory in _____

_____
_____
_____
_____

A Treasured Memory in _____

_____
_____
_____
_____

A Treasured Memory in _____

_____
_____
_____
_____

A Treasured Memory in _____

_____
_____
_____
_____

A Treasured Memory in _____

_____
_____
_____
_____

A Treasured Memory in _____

_____
_____
_____
_____

A Treasured Memory in _____
_____
_____
_____
_____
_____

A Treasured Memory in _____
_____
_____
_____
_____
_____

A Treasured Memory in _____
_____
_____
_____
_____
_____

A Treasured Memory in _____
_____
_____
_____
_____
_____

A Treasured Memory in _____
_____
_____
_____
_____
_____

A Treasured Memory in _____
_____
_____
_____
_____
_____

South America

Peru

☐ **Machu Picchu.** An Incan citadel set high in the Andes Mountains. Built in the 15th century and later abandoned, it's renowned for its sophisticated dry-stone walls that fuse huge blocks without the use of mortar, intriguing buildings that play on astronomical alignments and sweeping panoramic views. The best months of the year are late March through May and September through early November. During these months, it tends to be significantly less crowded with relatively good weather conditions.

Date Completed: _____

Ecuador

☐ **The Galápagos Islands.** The Galápagos Islands is a volcanic archipelago in the Pacific Ocean. It's considered one of the world's foremost destinations for wildlife-viewing. Seasons are split into cool and dry (June-November) and warm and wet (December-June), with the warmer season being the best time to visit for calmer seas and good underwater visibility.

Date Completed: _____

☐ **See the Blue-Footed Booby bird mating dance.**

Date Completed: _____

Chile

☐ **Easter Island.** A remote volcanic island in Polynesia. It's famed for archaeological sites, including nearly 900 monumental statues called moai, created by inhabitants during the 13th–16th centuries. The moai are carved human figures with oversized heads, often resting on massive stone pedestals called ahus. The best time to visit is during one of the shoulder seasons – April to June or October to December – as the climate is temperate and prices are more affordable.

Date Completed: _____

☐ **Trek the jagged coast of Chilean Patagonia.**

Date Completed: _____

Place I Visited _____

About the Culture
_____
_____
_____
_____
_____

What I Learned
_____
_____
_____
_____
_____

My Reflection
_____
_____
_____
_____
_____

A Treasured Memory
_____
_____
_____
_____
_____

A Treasured Memory
_____
_____
_____
_____
_____

Brazil

☐ **Christ the Redeemer in Rio de Janeiro.** A massive 98-foot tall Art Deco statue of Jesus Christ created by French sculptor Paul Landowski and built by Brazilian engineer Heitor da Silva Costa, in collaboration with French engineer Albert Caquot. The best time to go is early in the morning during the week, or late afternoon when there are few crowds, less heat and better visibility.

Date Completed: _____

☐ **Carnival in Rio De Janeiro.** Without a doubt, Carnival in Rio is the world's most famous party. While the city dances to the beat for days before it begins, official Carnival days are Saturday through Tuesday in late February. The highlight of Carnival is the Samba Parade, which is not to be missed!

Date Completed: _____

☐ **Stand on the equator line.**

Date Completed: _____

Bolivia

☐ **Salar de Uyuni.** The world's largest salt flat. It's the legacy of a prehistoric lake that went dry, leaving behind a desert-like, nearly 11,000-sq.-km. landscape of bright-white salt, rock formations and cacti-studded islands. Its otherworldly expanse can be observed from central Incahuasi Island. Though wildlife is rare in this unique ecosystem, it harbors many pink flamingos. For the best climate, visit between July and October. However, for an increased chance of seeing the reflective surfaces, you should visit between March and April.

Date Completed: _____

☐ **Lake Titicaca.** Literally just putting this on here because I am still a child and can't get over the name.

Date Completed: _____

Place I Visited _____

About the Culture
_____
_____
_____
_____
_____

What I Learned
_____
_____
_____
_____
_____

My Reflection
_____
_____
_____
_____
_____

A Treasured Memory
_____
_____
_____
_____
_____

A Treasured Memory
_____
_____
_____
_____
_____

Other South American Countries

- [ ] Argentina
- [ ] Bolivia
- [ ] Columbia
- [ ] Guyana
- [ ] Paraguay
- [ ] Suriname
- [ ] Venezuela

Places I would like to go in South America

A Treasured Memory in _____
_____
_____
_____
_____

A Treasured Memory in _____
_____
_____
_____
_____
_____

A Treasured Memory in _____
_____
_____
_____
_____
_____

A Treasured Memory in _____
_____
_____
_____
_____

A Treasured Memory in _____
_____
_____
_____
_____

A Treasured Memory in _____
_____
_____
_____
_____

Antarctica

☐ **Polar Plunge.** The Polar Plunge sometimes takes place onshore or, in many cases, from the gangway or Zodiac. Participants wear a tethered harness and plunge into the icy waters from the side of a raft. The best time to take a polar plunge in Antarctica is in December. In preparation for a plunge, first take an ice-cold shower. This will help your system adjust to what lies ahead.
Date Completed: _____

☐ **Interact with Penguins.** Penguins are the number one attraction for many visitors to Antarctica. You're pretty much guaranteed to see them up close as long as you go on a boat tour. There are restrictions, as you have to stay five yards away from the birds in order to not stress them out. The best time of year to visit is during the Antarctic summer from November to March, when you'll see Antarctica's wildlife at its busiest and benefit from up to 24 hours of daylight.
Date Completed: _____

☐ **See an Iceberg.** I think this is self-explanatory and everyone knows what an iceberg is if you have seen Titanic. Antarctica holds some of the biggest icebergs so it will be the best to see them there. Most weigh over 300 billion tons!
Date Completed: _____

Places I would like to go in Antarctica

☐ _____ ☐ _____
☐ _____ ☐ _____
☐ _____ ☐ _____
☐ _____ ☐ _____
☐ _____ ☐ _____
☐ _____ ☐ _____
☐ _____ ☐ _____
☐ _____ ☐ _____
☐ _____ ☐ _____
☐ _____ ☐ _____
☐ _____ ☐ _____
☐ _____ ☐ _____
☐ _____ ☐ _____

Place I Visited _____

About the Culture

What I Learned

My Reflection

A Treasured Memory

A Treasured Memory

Books to Read

While you are enjoying your vacation traveling the world, what better time to catch up on your reading. I know the last section was a lot to devour, but this section should keep you busy while you vacation is South Belize or any beautiful tropical climate, or cuddled up on your couch, or even if you want to start a book club. This isn't just about the books that shaped our time, but the authors who we have grown to love.

When She is Feeling Nostalgic

- ☐ **Wuthering Heights - Emily Brontë.** Taking its name from the Yorkshire farmhouse where the story is set, we fall into the intense love story of Catherine Earnshaw and Heathcliff. Violent, beautiful and all against the wild backdrop of the Yorkshire Moors, it's one of the most famous stories of all time.

- ☐ **Don Juan - Lord Byron.** Byron's exuberant masterpiece tells of the adventures of Don Juan, beginning with his illicit love affair at the age of sixteen in his native Spain and his subsequent exile to Italy. Following a dramatic shipwreck, his exploits take him to Greece, where he is sold as a slave, and to Russia, where he becomes a favorite of the Empress Catherine.

- ☐ **She: A History of Adventure - H.R. Haggard.** Legends tell of an ancient sorceress who has learned the secrets of immortality. She rules over a lost people deep in unexplored Africa. She can slay at a glance, and her beauty is so legendary that no man can look upon her and keep his own will. In it, Leo Vincey learns of a quest that has haunted his family for generations. He is to go find this all-powerful woman, and discover the secret of eternal life.

- ☐ **Age of Innocence - Edith Wharton.** There's a reason why Wharton was the first female writer to win the Pulitzer Prize. Newland Archer, gentleman lawyer and heir to one of New York City's best families, is happily anticipating a highly desirable marriage to the sheltered and beautiful May Welland. Yet he finds reason to doubt his choice of bride after the appearance of Countess Ellen Olenska, May's exotic, beautiful 30-year-old cousin, who has been living in Europe.

- ☐ **Vanity Fair - William Makepeace Thackeray.** The story is framed as a puppet play, told by an unreliable narrator, that presents the story of Becky Sharp and Emmy Sedley and the people in their lives as they struggle through the Napoleonic Wars. The story itself is a satire of the lives of the Victorian English of a certain class. As part of his satirical bent, Thackeray made a point to make each character flawed, so that there are no "heroes" in the book.

- ☐ **Lolita - Vladimir Nabokov.** *Lolita* immediately became a cause célèbre because of the freedom and sophistication with which it handled the unusual erotic predilections of its protagonist. Awe and exhilaration along with heartbreak and mordant wit abound in this account of the aging

Humbert Humbert's obsessive, devouring, and doomed passion for the nymphet Dolores. It is a meditation on love - as outrage and hallucination, madness and transformation.

☐ *Pride and Prejudice* - **Jane Austen.** The story follows Elizabeth Bennet as she deals with issues of manners, upbringing, morality, education, and marriage in landed-gentry society.

☐ *The Great Gatsby* - **F. Scott Fitzgerald.** The story of the mysteriously wealthy Jay Gatsby and his love for the beautiful Daisy Buchanan, of lavish parties on Long Island at a time when *The New York Times* noted "gin was the national drink and sex the national obsession," it is an exquisitely crafted tale of America in the 1920s.

☐ *Great Expectations* - **Charles Dickens.** A bildungsroman which depicts the personal growth and development of an orphan nicknamed Pip. It is set in London in the early to mid-1800s. Great Expectations is full of extreme imagery – poverty, prison ships and chains, and fights to the death – and has a colorful cast of characters who have entered popular culture.

☐ *Anna Karenina* - **Leo Tolstoy.** One of the strongest female characters to ever grace a novel's pages, Anna Karenina leads us through her complicated life of love, death, affairs, and ultimately tragedy.

☐ *Jane Eyre* - **Charlotte Brontë.** Jane Eyre and Rochester, one of the greatest love stories ever told. Set against the backdrop of the Yorkshire moors, Eyre becomes the governess to the terrifying Mr. Rochester. But there's a whole lot more to him than first meets the eye.

☐ *The Count of Monte Cristo* - **Alexandre Dumas.** An expansive adventure novel with a huge cast of characters, all revolving around the young sailor Edmond Dantès. Wrongfully accused of aiding the exiled Napoleon, Dantès is arrested on the day of his wedding and imprisoned. He survives years of cramped confinement and eventually befriends another prisoner, an Italian who knows the location of a treasure on the island of Monte Cristo. After an intrepid escape, Dantès utilizes his new fortune to extract revenge from his enemies, pursuing those who imprisoned him to a bitter end for all concerned.

When She is feeling like an Activist

☐ *The Prince* - **Nicolo Machiavelli.** Ever wonder where the term Machiavellian came from? Someone who is Machiavellian is sneaky, cunning, and lacking a moral code, and who also coined the idea of "the end justifies the means" behavior, especially among politicians. *The Prince* is one of the first works of modern political philosophy, in which the effective truth is taken to be more important than any abstract ideal. It also helped make "Old Nick" an English term for the devil, and even contributed to the modern negative connotations of the words "politics" and "politician" in western countries.

☐ *The Diary of a Young Girl* - **Anne Frank.** The real-life record of a remarkable Jewish girl who was in hiding for 2 years during the Nazi occupation in the Netherlands. Her triumphant humanity in the face of unfathomable deprivation and fear has made the book one of the most enduring documents of our time.

☐ ***The Art of War* – Sun Tzu.** Compiled more than 2,000 years ago by a mysterious warrior-philosopher as a study of the anatomy of organizations in conflict, *The Art of War* applies to competition and conflict in general, on every level from the interpersonal to the international. Its aim is invincibility, victory without battle, and unassailable strength through understanding the physics, politics, and psychology of conflict.

☐ ***Atlas Shrugged* – Ayn Rand.** The story tells of a scrap heap within an abandoned factory that holds the greatest invention in history, which lies dormant and unused. By what fatal error of judgment has its value gone unrecognized, its brilliant inventor punished rather than rewarded for his efforts? In defense of those greatest of human qualities that have made civilization possible, one man sets out to show what would happen to the world if all the heroes of innovation and industry went on strike.

When She is Feeling Namaste

☐ ***The Power of Now* – Eckhart Tolle.** To make the journey into *The Power of Now* you need to leave your analytical mind and its false created self, the ego, behind. Access to the Now is everywhere – in the body, the silence, and the space all around you. These are the keys to enter a state of inner peace. They can be used to bring you into the Now, the present moment, where problems do not exist. It is here you find your joy and are able to embrace your true self. This work of nonfiction is about discovering that you are already complete and perfect.

☐ ***The Seven Spiritual Laws of Success* – Deepak Chopra.** Looking for a practical guide to the fulfillment of your dreams? Based on natural laws which govern all of creation, this book shatters the myth that success is the result of hard work, exacting plans, or driving ambition.

☐ ***Journey of Souls* – Michael Newton.** *Journey of Souls* presents the first-hand accounts of 29 people placed in a "superconscious" state of awareness. While in deep hypnosis, the subjects movingly describe what happened to them between lives. They reveal graphic details about what the spirit world is really like, where we go and what we do as souls, and why we come back in certain bodies. This book describes when and where you learn to recognize soulmates on earth, what happens to "disturbed" souls, the purpose of life and the manifestation of a "creator". This book literally changed my life and how I view everything. It makes so much sense regardless of what religion you are or what you believe.

☐ ***The Four Agreements* – Don Miguel Ruiz.** In *The Four Agreements*, don Miguel Ruiz reveals the source of self-limiting beliefs that rob us of joy and create needless suffering. Based on ancient Toltec wisdom, it offers a powerful code of conduct that can rapidly transform our lives to a new experience of freedom, true happiness, and love.

☐ ***How to Win Friends and Influence People* – Dale Carnegie.** For over 60 years the rock-solid, time-tested advice has carried thousands of now-famous people up the ladder of success in their business and personal lives. Learn: The six ways to make people like you, the twelve ways to win people to your way of thinking, the nine ways to change people without arousing resentment, and much, much more.

☐ ***Chicken Soup for the Woman's Soul* – Jack Canfield.** What bonds all women are our mutual experiences of loving and learning, feeling the tenderness of love, forging lifelong friendships, pursuing a chosen career, giving birth to new life, juggling the responsibilities of job and family and more. This shining collection offers inspiration and comfort in special chapters on marriage, motherhood, aging, attitude, self-esteem, and higher wisdom.

☐ *The Alchemist* - **Paulo Coelho.** This story, dazzling in its simplicity and wisdom, is about an Andalusian shepherd boy named Santiago who travels from his homeland in Spain to the Egyptian desert in search of treasure buried in the Pyramids. Along the way he meets a Gypsy woman, a man who calls himself king, and an Alchemist, all of whom point Santiago in the direction of his quest. No one knows what the treasure is, or if Santiago will be able to surmount the obstacles along the way. What starts out as a journey to find worldly goods turns into a meditation on the treasures found within.

When She Needs a Laugh

☐ *Bridget Jones's Diary* - **Helen Fielding.** The ultimate single woman's companion, Fielding shares the diary of ever-single Bridget Jones and her doomed love life. There are tears, love, weight loss and weight gain, a whole lot of vodka and a serious amount of laugh-out-loud moments.

☐ *She's Come Undone* - **Wally Lamb.** Meet Dolores Price. She's thirteen, wise-mouthed but wounded, having bid her childhood goodbye. Beached like a whale in front of her bedroom TV, she spends the next few years nourishing herself with the Mallomars, potato chips and Pepsi her anxious mother supplies. When she finally rolls into young womanhood at 257 pounds, Dolores is no stronger and life is no kinder. But this time she's determined to rise to the occasion and give herself one more chance before *really* going belly up. In this extraordinary coming-of-age odyssey, Wally Lamb invites us to hitch a wild ride on a journey of love, pain and renewal with the most heartbreakingly comical heroine to come along in years.

☐ *The Grass Is Always Greener Over the Septic Tank* - **Erma Bombeck.** It's the exposé to end all exposés—the truth about the suburbs: where they planted trees and crabgrass came up, where they planted the schools and taxes came up, where they died of old age trying to merge onto the freeway and where they finally got sex out of the schools and back into the gutters.

When She is Feeling Mysterious

☐ *A Study in Scarlet* - **Arthur Conan Doyle.** Yes, ladies, this is the original Sherlock Holmes novel. You're welcome for that trivia answer. After returning from the Second Anglo-Afghan War, Dr. John. H. Watson begins to seek out someone to share a living space with. It is then that he is introduced to Mr. Sherlock Holmes, and thus begins the famous relationship between the master detective and the good doctor. Upon hearing of a murder committed in an abandoned house, Dr. Watson convinces the reluctant Sherlock to investigate.

☐ *And Then There Were None* - **Agatha Christie.** Perhaps the best-known murder mystery of all time, *And Then There Were None* absolutely epitomizes suspense. Ten strangers meet on an isolated British isle at the behest of their oddly absent hosts. But when they start dying off one by one — in disturbing parallels to a children's nursery rhyme — they realize that this is no vacation, but a collective execution. Christie brilliantly immerses the reader in the fear and paranoia of the guests as they try to determine who among them is the killer… before their time runs out.

When She is in the Mood for Love

- ☐ *A Spy in the House of Love* - **Anaïs Nin.** Beautiful, bored and bourgeoise, Sabina leads a double life inspired by her relentless desire for brief encounters with near-strangers. Fired into faithlessness by a desperate longing for sexual fulfillment, she weaves a sensual web of deceit across New York.

- ☐ *Venus in Furs* - **Leopold von Sacher-Masoch.** And you thought E.L. James was a badass… this is literally the man who penned the term masochism. I knew you were wondering, so you're welcome. Drawn in part from his own life experiences, Sacher-Masoch's novel develops an eroticism unlike any other. The book's protagonist, Severin, is so infatuated and obsessed with the object of his desire, Wanda, that he asks to be her slave.

- ☐ *Lace* - **Shirley Conran.** The original bonkbuster, Shirley Conran shocked readers everywhere when she released her raunchy tale of four young women and their sexual exploits over the years, involving everything from secret pregnancies to some very interesting sex acts involving goldfish... Addictive. Before Sex and The City there was *Lace*.

- ☐ *Skye O'Malley* - **Beatrice Small.** One of the pioneers in Erotica with her most delicious series. Indomitable and bold in an era of royalty and rogues, the character of Skye O'Malley is a woman who embraces her unbridled sensuality as valiantly as she fights for her children, her lovers, her empire. Though Skye is the object of every man's fantasy, only a handful have had the thrill of tasting her enticing passions–men whose own daring adventures match her exotic forays into a world of lust, longing, and remarkable destiny. Skye's is a stunning tale that reaches from the emerald hills of Ireland to the lush palaces of Algiers, to the helm of a shipping empire where she will wage her greatest battle for love and vengeance against the crown itself.

When She Needs to Be a Girl Again

- ☐ *Alice's Adventures in Wonderland and Through the Looking Glass* - **Lewis Carroll.** The story of Alice, an inquisitive young heroine who falls through a rabbit hole and into a whimsical world, has captured the hearts of readers of all ages. Alice is accompanied on her journey of trials and tribulations by the frantic White Rabbit, the demented and terrifying Queen of Hearts, the intriguing Mad Hatter, and many other eccentric characters.

- ☐ *Little Women* - **Louisa May Alcott.** *Little Women* has long been one of the most enduringly beloved classics of children's literature, as popular with adults as it is with young readers. Generations have been entranced by the adventures of the four March sisters, each with their distinct and realistic virtues and flaws: tomboyish, ambitious Jo; frail and sweet Beth; beautiful, confident Meg; and artistic, willful Amy. With their patient mother, Marmee, they survive the hardships of the Civil War and the dramas and tragedies of family life.

- ☐ *Anne of Green Gables* - **L.M. Montgomery.** It chronicles the coming of age of a young orphan girl, from the fictional community of Bolingbroke, Nova Scotia. The story begins with her arrival at the Prince Edward Island farm of Miss Marilla Cuthbert and Mr. Matthew Cuthbert, siblings in their fifties and sixties, who had decided to adopt a young boy to help out on the farm. However, through a misunderstanding, the orphanage sends Anne Shirley instead. While the Cuthberts are at first determined to return Anne to the orphanage, after a few days they decide instead to keep her. Anne is an imaginative and energetic young girl, who quickly befriends Diana Barry at the local country school, becomes rivals with classmate Gilbert Blythe who teases her about her red hair, and has unfortunate run-ins with the unpleasant Pye sisters.

☐ *Matilda* - **Roald Dahl.** Matilda is a sweet, exceptional young girl, but her parents think she's just a nuisance. She expects school to be different but there she has to face Miss Trunchbull, a kid-hating terror of a headmistress. When Matilda is attacked by Trunchbull she suddenly discovers she has a remarkable power with which to fight back. It'll take a superhuman genius to give Miss Trunchbull what she deserves and Matilda may be just the one to do it!

☐ *Are You There God? It's Me, Margaret.* - **Judy Blume.** Faced with the difficulties of growing up and choosing a religion, a twelve-year-old girl talks over her problems with her own private God.

☐ *The Giver* - **Lois Lowry.** The 1994 Newbery Medal winner has become one of the most influential novels of our time. The haunting story centers around twelve-year-old Jonas, who lives in a seemingly ideal, if colorless, world of conformity and contentment. Not until he is given his life assignment as the Receiver of Memory does he begin to understand the dark, complex secrets behind his fragile community.

When She Needs Advice

☐ *The Art of Seduction* - **Robert Greene.** When raised to the level of art, seduction, an indirect and subtle form of power, has toppled empires, won elections and enslaved great minds. Immerse yourself in the twenty-four maneuvers and strategies of the seductive process.

☐ *The Female Brain* - **Louann Brizendine M.D.** Why are women more verbal than men? Why do women remember details of fights that men can't remember at all? Why do women tend to form deeper bonds with their female friends than men do with their male counterparts? These and other questions have stumped both sexes throughout the ages. Now, pioneering neuropsychiatrist Louann Brizendine, M.D., brings together the latest findings to show how the unique structure of the female brain determines how women think, and how they communicate.

☐ *The Male Brain* - **Louann Brizendine M.D.** If you read one, you might as well read the other. Dr. Louann Brizendine turns her attention to the male brain in this book, showing how, through every phase of life, the "male reality" is fundamentally different from the female one.

☐ *He's Just Not That Into You* - **Greg Behrendt & Liz Tuccillo.** Why didn't he call you back? Why doesn't he talk to your friends? Why does he keep putting off your dates? This book has the answers. It is a hilarious, playful, honest explanation of male behavior from a writer and consultant of *Sex and the City*. Stop wasting your time chasing after men who aren't into you, and find men who are!

☐ *The Five Love Languages* – **Dr. Gary Chapman.** This book identifies five basic languages of love and then guides couples towards a better understanding of each other's unique love languages. Learn to effectively love and truly feel loved in return.

When She Wants A Memoir Moment

☐ *I Know Why the Caged Bird Sings* – **Maya Angelou.** Here is a book as joyous, painful, mysterious and memorable as childhood itself. *I Know Why the Caged Bird Sings* captures the longing of lonely children, the brute insult of bigotry, and the wonder of words that can make the world right.

☐ *Crazy Salad & Scribble Scribble: Some Things about Women & Notes on the Media* – **Nora Ephron.** As one of the most influential female filmmakers of our time, we all need to feel inspired by the one and only. A collection of Nora Ephron's most brilliant essays explores everything from feminism to the media, via beauty and politics. Smart, hilarious and brilliant, it's Ephron at her very best.

When She's a Bad Ass

☐ *The Awakening* – **Kate Chopin.** Set in New Orleans and on the Louisiana Gulf coast at the end of the 19th century, the plot centers on Edna Pontellier and her struggle to reconcile her increasingly unorthodox views on femininity and motherhood with the prevailing social attitudes of the American South during the turn-of-the-century. It is one of the earliest American novels that focuses on women's issues without condescension.

☐ *Wilderness Tips* – **Margaret Atwood.** Anything by Margaret Atwood is amazing. I specifically like her short stories. *Wilderness Tips* made me want to adapt it into a movie. I think it was the first story.

☐ *A Room of One's Own* – **Virginia Woolf.** In *A Room of One's Own*, Virginia Woolf imagines that Shakespeare had a sister—a sister equal to Shakespeare in talent, and equal in genius, but whose legacy is radically different.

☐ *The Bell Jar* – **Sylvia Plath.** It may have been the only novel she ever wrote, but under the guise of 'Victoria Lucas', poet Plath brilliantly captured the heartbreaking loneliness of Esther Greenwood, who despite her early success interning at a New York fashion magazine, finds herself spiraling into severe depression. It's even more heartbreaking when you discover the novel was partly autobiographical.

☐ *The Complete Poems of Emily Dickinson* – **Emily Dickinson.** Only eleven of Emily Dickinson's poems were published prior to her death in 1886; the startling originality of her work doomed it to obscurity in her lifetime. Early posthumous published collections -- some of them featuring liberally "edited" versions of the poems -- did not fully and accurately represent Dickinson's bold experiments in prosody, her tragic vision, and the range of her intellectual and emotional explorations.

More Books to Read

- [ ] _____ By: _____
- [ ] _____ By: _____
- [ ] _____ By: _____
- [ ] _____ By: _____
- [ ] _____ By: _____
- [ ] _____ By: _____
- [ ] _____ By: _____
- [ ] _____ By: _____
- [ ] _____ By: _____
- [ ] _____ By: _____
- [ ] _____ By: _____
- [ ] _____ By: _____
- [ ] _____ By: _____
- [ ] _____ By: _____
- [ ] _____ By: _____
- [ ] _____ By: _____
- [ ] _____ By: _____
- [ ] _____ By: _____
- [ ] _____ By: _____
- [ ] _____ By: _____
- [ ] _____ By: _____
- [ ] _____ By: _____
- [ ] _____ By: _____
- [ ] _____ By: _____
- [ ] _____ By: _____
- [ ] _____ By: _____
- [ ] _____ By: _____
- [ ] _____ By: _____
- [ ] _____ By: _____
- [ ] _____ By: _____

Movies to Watch

From the most iconic lines in film history, to the best female-driven scripts, to the classics these are the must-see movies. Most of the classic films make their rounds on the Turner Classic Movie network, or TCM. I know this one you will check off a lot as they are cult classics that every female has in her repertoire.

When She's Feeling Nostalgic
(classics everyone should watch)

☐ **Adam's Rib (1949)**
Starring: Spencer Tracy and Katharine Hepburn.
Plot: Domestic and professional tensions mount when a husband and wife work as opposing lawyers in a case involving a woman who shot her husband.

☐ **All About Eve (1950)**
Starring: Bette Davis and Anne Baxter
Plot: An ingénue insinuates herself into the lives of an established but aging stage actress and her circle of theater friends.

☐ **Born Yesterday (1950)**
Starring: Judy Holliday and William Holden
Plot: A tycoon hires a tutor to teach his lover proper etiquette, with unexpected results.

☐ **Breakfast at Tiffany's (1961)**
Starring: Audrey Hepburn and George Peppard
Plot: A young New York socialite becomes interested in a young man who has moved into her apartment building, but her past threatens to get in the way.

☐ **Dr. Zhivago (1965)**
Starring: Omar Sharif and Julie Christie
Plot: The life of a Russian physician and poet who, although married to another, falls in love with a political activist's wife and experiences hardship during World War I.

☐ **Gone with the Wind (1939)**
Starring: Clark Gable and Vivien Leigh
Plot: A manipulative woman and a roguish man conduct a turbulent romance during the American Civil War and Reconstruction periods.

☐ **How to Marry a Millionaire (1953)**
Starring: Marilyn Monroe, Betty Grable and Lauren Bacall
Plot: Three women set out to find eligible millionaires to marry, but find true love in the process.

☐ **It's a Wonderful Life (1946)**
Starring: James Stewart and Donna Reed
Plot: An angel is sent from Heaven to help a desperately frustrated businessman by showing him what life would have been like if he had never existed.

☐ **North by Northwest (1959)**
Starring: Cary Grant
Plot: A New York City advertising executive goes on the run after being mistaken for a government agent by a group of foreign spies.

☐ **The Rocky Horror Picture Show (1975)**
Starring: Tim Curry and Susan Sarandon
Plot: A newly engaged couple have a breakdown in an isolated area and must pay a call to the bizarre residence of Dr. Frank N. Furter.

☐ **The Seven-Year Itch (1955)**
Starring: Marilyn Monroe, Tom Ewell and Evelyn Keyes
Plot: When his family goes away for the summer, a hitherto faithful husband with an overactive imagination is tempted by a beautiful neighbor.

When She's Feeling Tough
(Hard kicking female leads)

☐ **The Devil Wears Prada (2011)**
Starring: Anne Hathaway and Meryl Streep
Plot: A graduate lands a job as an assistant to a demanding editor-in-chief of a fashion magazine.

☐ **Basic Instinct (1992)**
Starring: Michael Douglas and Sharon Stone
Plot: A police detective investigates a brutal murder that might involve a seductive novelist.

☐ **Erin Brockovich (2000)**
Starring: Julia Roberts and Albert Finney
Plot: Based on a true story. An unemployed single mother becomes a legal assistant and almost single-handedly brings down a California power company accused of polluting a city's water supply.

☐ **Fatal Attraction (1987)**
Starring: Michael Douglas and Glenn Close
Plot: A married man's one-night stand comes back to haunt him.

☐ **Misery (1990)**
Starring: Kathy Bates and James Caan
Plot: After an author is rescued by a fan, he realizes the care is only the beginning of a nightmare.

☐ **Norma Rae (1979)**
Starring: Sally Field and Beau Bridges
Plot: A young single mother and textile worker agrees to help unionize her mill despite the problems and dangers involved.

☐ **Steel Magnolias (1989)**
Starring: Shirley MacLaine, Olympia Dukakis and Sally Field
Plot: A young beautician, newly arrived in a small Louisiana town, finds work at the local salon where a small group of women share a close bond of friendship and welcome her into the fold.

☐ **Sunset Boulevard (1950)**
Starring: Gloria Swanson
Plot: A screenwriter develops a dangerous relationship with a faded film star determined to make a triumphant return.

☐ **Thelma and Louise (1991)**
Starring: Susan Sarandon and Geena Davis
Plot: Two best friends set out on an adventure, but it soon turns into a terrifying escape from the police.

☐ **Waiting to Exhale (1995)**
Starring: Whitney Houston, Angela Bassett and Loretta Devine
Plot: Based on Terry McMillan's novel, this film follows four very different African-American women and their relationships with men.

☐ **Who's Afraid of Virginia Woolf? (1966)**
Starring: Elizabeth Taylor, Richard Burton, and George Segal
Plot: A bitter, aging couple, with the help of alcohol, use their young houseguests to fuel anguish and emotional pain towards each other over the course of a distressing night.

☐ **9 to 5 (1980)**
Starring: Jane Fonda, Lily Tomlin and Dolly Parton
Plot: Three female employees of a sexist, egotistical, lying, hypocritical bigot find a way to turn the tables on him.

When She Needs A Good Laugh
(comedies)

☐ **Clueless (1995)**
Starring: Alicia Silverstone, Stacey Dash and Brittany Murphy
Plot: A rich high school student tries to boost a new pupil's popularity, but reckons without affairs of the heart getting in the way.

☐ **A League of their Own (1992)**
Starring: Tom Hanks and Geena Davis
Plot: Two sisters join a female professional baseball league and struggle to help it succeed.

☐ **Legally Blonde (2001)**
Starring: Reese Witherspoon, Luke Wilson and Selma Blair
Plot: Elle Woods, a fashionable sorority queen is dumped by her boyfriend and decides to follow him to law school. While there, she figures out that there is more to her than just looks.

☐ **Mean Girls (2004)**
Starring: Lindsay Lohan and Rachel McAdams
Plot: Cady Heron is a hit with The Plastics, the A-list girl clique, until she makes the mistake of falling for Aaron Samuels, the ex-boyfriend of alpha Plastic Regina George.

☐ **My Best Friend's Wedding (1997)**
Starring: Julia Roberts, Dermot Mulroney and Cameron Diaz
Plot: When a woman's long-time friend reveals he's engaged, she realizes she loves him herself and sets out to get him, only days before the wedding.

☐ **Monty Python and the Holy Grail (1975)**
Starring: John Cleese
Plot: King Arthur and his Knights of the Round Table embark on a surreal, low-budget search for the Holy Grail, encountering many, very silly obstacles.

☐ **Romy and Michele's High School Reunion (1997)**
Starring: Mira Sorvino, Lisa Kudrow and Janeane Garofalo
Plot: Two dim-witted, inseparable friends hit the road for their ten-year high school reunion and concoct an elaborate lie about their lives in order to impress their classmates.

☐ **Singles (1992)**
Starring: Bridget Fonda, Campbell Scott and Kyra Sedgwick
Plot: A group of twenty-something friends, most of whom live in the same apartment complex, search for love and success in grunge-era Seattle.

☐ **Sixteen Candles (1984)**
Starring: Molly Ringwald, Anthony Michael Hall and Justin Henry
Plot: A girl's "sweet" sixteenth birthday becomes anything but special when she suffers from every embarrassment possible.

☐ **Some Like it Hot (1959)**
Starring: Marilyn Monroe, Tony Curtis and Jack Lemmon
Plot: When two male musicians witness a mob hit, they flee the state in an all-female band disguised as women, but further complications set in.

☐ **10 Things I Hate About You (1999)**
Starring: Heath Ledger, Julia Stiles and Joseph Gordon-Levitt
Plot: A pretty, popular teenager isn't allowed to go out on a date until her ill-tempered older sister does.

When She Needs A Good Cry
(dramas)

☐ **The Breakfast Club (1985)**
Starring: Emilio Estevez and Molly Ringwald
Plot: Five high school students meet in Saturday detention and discover they have a lot more in common than they thought.

☐ **Citizen Kane (1941)**
Starring: Orson Welles
Plot: Following the death of publishing tycoon Charles Foster Kane, reporters scramble to uncover the meaning of his final utterance: 'Rosebud'.

☐ **The Color Purple (1985)**
Starring: Danny Glover, Whoopi Goldberg and Oprah Winfrey
Plot: An African-American woman struggles to find her identity after suffering abuse from her father.

☐ **Eternal Sunshine of the Spotless Mind (2004)**
Starring: Jim Carrey and Kate Winslet
Plot: When their relationship turns sour, a couple undergoes a medical procedure to have each other erased from their memories.

☐ **Fight Club (1999)**
Starring: Brad Pitt and Edward Norton
Plot: An insomniac office worker and a devil-may-care soap maker form an underground fight club that evolves into something much, much more.

☐ **Fried Green Tomatoes (1991)**
Starring: Kathy Bates, Jessica Tandy and Mary Stuart Masterson
Plot: A housewife who is unhappy with her life befriends an old lady in a nursing home and is enthralled by the tales she tells of people she used to know.

☐ **The Graduate (1967)**
Starring: Anne Bancroft and Dustin Hoffman
Plot: A disillusioned graduate finds himself torn between his older lover and her daughter.

☐ **Guess Who's Coming to Dinner (1967)**
Starring: Spencer Tracy, Sidney Poitier and Katherine Hepburn
Plot: A couple's attitudes are challenged when their daughter introduces them to her African-American fiancé.

☐ **Mystic Pizza (1988)**
Starring: Annabeth Gish, Julia Roberts and Lili Taylor
Plot: Three teenage girls come of age while working at a pizza parlor in a Connecticut town.

☐ **Network (1976)**
Starring: Faye Dunaway, William Holden and Peter Finch
Plot: A television network cynically exploits a deranged former anchor's ravings and revelations about the news media for its own profit.

☐ **Now and Then (1995)**
Starring: Christina Ricci, Demi Moore and Rosie O'Donnell
Plot: Four 12-year-old girls grow up together during an eventful small-town summer in 1970.

☐ **Rocky (1976)**
Starring: Sylvester Stallone and Talia Shire
Plot: A small-time boxer gets a supremely rare chance to fight a heavy-weight champion in a bout in which he strives to go the distance for his self-respect.

☐ **The Shawshank Redemption (1994)**
Starring: Tim Robbins and Morgan Freeman
Plot: Two imprisoned men bond over a number of years, finding solace and eventual redemption through acts of common decency.

☐ **Splendor in the Grass (1961)**
Starring: Natalie Wood, Warren Beatty and Pat Hingle
Plot: A fragile Kansas girl's love for a handsome young man from the town's most powerful family drives her to heartbreak and madness.

☐ **Terms of Endearment (1983)**
Starring: Shirley MacLaine, Debra Winger and Jack Nicholson
Plot: The film follows hard-to-please Aurora looking for love, and her daughter's family problems.

When She Needs to Believe in Love
(romance)

☐ **An Affair to Remember (1957)**
Starring: Cary Grant and Deborah Kerr
Plot: A couple falls in love and agrees to meet in six months at the Empire State Building - but will it happen?

☐ **Annie Hall (1977)**
Starring: Woody Allen and Diane Keaton
Plot: Neurotic New York comedian Alvy Singer falls in love with the ditzy Annie Hall.

☐ **The Awful Truth (1937)**
Starring: Irene Dunne and Cary Grant
Plot: Unfounded suspicions lead a married couple to begin divorce proceedings, whereupon they start undermining each other's attempts to find new romance.

☐ **Casablanca (1942)**
Starring: Humphrey Bogart and Ingrid Bergman
Plot: A cynical American expatriate struggles to decide whether or not he should help his former lover and her fugitive husband escape French Morocco.

☐ **Ghost (1990)**
Starring: Patrick Swayze, Demi Moore and Whoopi Goldberg
Plot: After a young man is murdered, his spirit stays behind to warn his lover of impending danger, with the help of a reluctant psychic.

☐ **His Girl Friday (1940)**
Starring: Cary Grant and Rosalind Russell
Plot: A newspaper editor uses every trick in the book to keep his ace reporter ex-wife from remarrying.

☐ **Love Actually (2003)**
Starring: Hugh Grant, Martine McCutcheon and Liam Neeson
Plot: The film follows the lives of eight very different couples as they deal with their love lives in various loosely interrelated tales, all set during a frantic month before Christmas in London, England.

☐ **Move Over, Darling (1963)**
Starring: Doris Day and James Garner
Plot: After having been lost at sea for several years, a missing wife thought long dead returns just after her husband has remarried.

☐ **My Big Fat Greek Wedding (2002)**
Starring: Nia Vardalos, John Corbett and Michael Constantine
Plot: A young Greek woman falls in love with a non-Greek and struggles to get her family to accept him while she comes to terms with her heritage and cultural identity.

☐ **The Notebook (2004)**
Starring: Ryan Gosling and Rachel McAdams
Plot: A poor yet passionate young man falls in love with a rich young woman, giving her a sense of freedom, but they are soon separated because of their social differences.

☐ **Notting Hill (1999)**
Starring: Hugh Grant and Julia Roberts
Plot: The life of a simple bookshop owner changes when he meets the most famous film star in the world.

☐ **Pillow Talk (1959)**
Starring: Rock Hudson and Doris Day
Plot: A man and a woman who share a party line cannot stand each other, but he has fun romancing her with his voice disguised.

☐ **Pretty in Pink (1986)**
Starring: Molly Ringwald, Jon Cryer and Andrew McCarthy
Plot: A poor girl must choose between the affections of dating her childhood sweetheart or a rich but sensitive playboy.

☐ **Pretty Woman (1990)**
Starring: Richard Gere and Julia Roberts
Plot: A businessman hires a beautiful prostitute for a short-term romp, but ends up falling for her.

☐ **The Princess Bride (1987)**
Starring: Cary Elwes, Mandy Patinkin and Robin Wright
Plot: While home sick in bed, a young boy's grandfather reads him the story of a farmboy-turned-pirate who encounters numerous obstacles in his quest to be reunited with his true love.

☐ **Now, Voyager (1942)**
Starring: Bette Davis, Paul Henreid and Claude Rains
Plot: A frumpy spinster blossoms under therapy and becomes an elegant, independent woman.

☐ **Random Harvest (1942)**
Starring: Ronald Colman, Greer Garson and Philip Dorn
Plot: An amnesiac World War I veteran falls in love with a music hall star, only to suffer an accident which restores his original memories but erases his post-war life.

☐ **Roman Holiday (1953)**
Starring: Gregory Peck, Audrey Hepburn and Eddie Albert
Plot: A bored and sheltered princess escapes her guardians and falls in love with an American newsman in Rome.

☐ **Sleepless in Seattle (1993)**
Starring: Tom Hanks, Meg Ryan and Ross Malinger
Plot: A recently widowed man's son calls a radio talk-show in an attempt to find his father a partner. Is there anything better than a Tom Hanks/Meg Ryan movie, I mean, honestly?

☐ **Sweet November (2001)**
Starring: Keanu Reeves and Charlize Theron
Plot: A workaholic executive and an unconventional woman agree to a personal relationship for a short period. In this short period, she changes his life.

☐ **To Catch a Thief (1955)**
Starring: Cary Grant, Grace Kelly and Jessie Royce Landis
Plot: A retired jewel thief sets out to prove his innocence after being suspected of returning to his former occupation.

☐ **The Way We Were (1973)**
Starring: Barbra Streisand, Robert Redford and Bradford Dillman
Plot: Two disparate people have a wonderful romance, but their political views and convictions drive them apart.

☐ **When a Man Loves a Woman (1994)**
Starring: Meg Ryan, Andy Garcia and Ellen Burstyn
Plot: The seemingly perfect relationship between a man and his wife is tested as a result of her alcoholism.

☐ **When Harry Met Sally (1989)**
Starring: Billy Crystal, Meg Ryan and Carrie Fisher
Plot: Harry and Sally have known each other for years and are very good friends, but they fear sex would ruin the friendship.

☐ **While You Were Sleeping (1995)**
Starring: Sandra Bullock, Bill Pullman and Peter Gallagher
Plot: A hopeless romantic Chicago Transit Authority token collector is mistaken for the fiancée of a coma patient.

☐ **9 and ½ Weeks (1986)**
Starring: Mickey Rourke, Kim Basinger and Margaret Whitton
Plot: A woman becomes involved with a man she barely knows. Complications develop during their sexual escapades.

When She Needs a Thrill
(Suspense)

☐ **Bonnie and Clyde (1967)**
Starring: Warren Beatty and Faye Dunaway
Plot: Bored waitress Bonnie Parker falls in love with an ex-con named Clyde Barrow and together they start a violent crime spree through the country, stealing cars and robbing banks.

☐ **Chinatown (1974)**
Starring: Jack Nicholson and Faye Dunaway
Plot: A private detective hired to expose an adulterer finds himself caught up in a web of deceit, corruption and murder.

☐ **Die Hard (1988)**
Starring: Bruce Willis and Allan Rickman
Plot: An NYPD officer tries to save his wife and several others taken hostage by German terrorists during a Christmas party at the Nakatomi Plaza in Los Angeles.

☐ **Double Indemnity (1944)**
Starring: Fred MacMurray, Barbara Stanwyck and Edward G. Robinson
Plot: An insurance rep gets talked into a murder/insurance fraud scheme by a sexy housewife.

☐ **Fargo (1996)**
Starring: William H. Macy, Frances McDormand and Steve Buscemi
Plot: Jerry Lundegaard's inept crime falls apart due to his and his henchmen's bungling and the persistent police work of the quite pregnant Marge Gunderson.

☐ **The Godfather Part 1 and 2 (1972)**
Starring: Marlon Brando, Al Pacino and James Caan
Plot: The aging patriarch of an organized crime dynasty transfers control of his clandestine empire to his reluctant son.

☐ **Goodfellas (1990)**
Starring: Robert De Niro, Ray Liotta and Joe Pesci
Plot: The story of Henry Hill and his life in the mob, covering his relationship with his wife Karen Hill and his mob partners Jimmy Conway and Tommy DeVito.

☐ **L.A. Confidential (1997)**
Starring: Kevin Spacey, Russell Crowe and Kim Basinger
Plot: As corruption grows in 1950s Los Angeles, three policemen -- one strait-laced, one brutally tough and one sleazy -- investigate a series of murders with their own brand of justice.

☐ **The Maltese Falcon (1941)**
Starring: Humphrey Bogart, Mary Astor and Gladys George
Plot: A private detective takes on a case that involves him with three eccentric criminals, a gorgeous liar and their quest for a priceless statuette.

☐ **Memento (2000)**
Starring: Guy Pearce, Carrie-Anne Moss and Joe Pantoliano
Plot: A man with short-term memory loss attempts to track down his wife's murderer.

☐ **The Matrix (1999)**
Starring: Keanu Reeves, Laurence Fishburne and Carrie-Anne Moss
Plot: A computer hacker learns from mysterious rebels about the true nature of his reality and his role in the war against its controllers.

☐ **Mulholland Drive (2001)**
Starring: Naomi Watts, Laura Harring, and Justin Theroux
Plot: After a car wreck on Mulholland Drive renders a woman amnesiac, she and a Hollywood-hopeful search for clues and answers in a twisting venture beyond dreams and reality.

☐ **Psycho (1960)**
Starring: Anthony Perkins and Janet Leigh
Plot: A Phoenix secretary embezzles forty thousand dollars from her employer's client, goes on the run, and checks into a remote motel run by a young man under the domination of his mother.

☐ **Pulp Fiction (1994)**
Starring: John Travolta, Uma Thurman and Samuel L. Jackson
Plot: The lives of two mob hitmen, a boxer, a gangster and his wife, and a pair of diner bandits intertwine in four tales of violence and redemption.

☐ **Run Lola Run (1998)**
Starring: Franka Potente, Moritz Bleibtreu and Herbert Knaup
Plot: After a botched money delivery, Lola has 20 minutes to come up with 100,000 Deutschmarks.

☐ **The Shining (1980)**
Starring: Jack Nicholson
Plot: A family heads to an isolated hotel for the winter where a sinister presence influences the father to become violence, while his psychic son sees horrific forebodings from both past and future.

☐ **The Usual Suspects (1995)**
Starring: Kevin Spacey, Gabriel Byrne and Chazz Palminteri
Plot: A sole survivor tells of the twisty events leading up to a horrific gun battle on a boat, which began when five criminals met at a seemingly random police lineup.

☐ **Vertigo (1958)**
Starring: James Stewart and Kim Novak
Plot: A former police detective juggles wrestling with his personal demons and becoming obsessed with a hauntingly beautiful woman.

When She Feels Like Belting Out A Tune
(musicals)

☐ **An American in Paris (1951)**
Starring: Gene Kelly and Leslie Caron
Plot: Three friends struggle to find work in Paris. Things become more complicated when two of them fall in love with the same woman.

☐ **Chicago (2002)**
Starring: Renée Zellweger and Catherine Zeta-Jones
Plot: Two death-row murderesses develop a fierce rivalry while competing for publicity, celebrity, and a sleazy lawyer's attention.

☐ **Dirty Dancing (1987)**
Starring: Patrick Swayze and Jennifer Grey
Plot: Spending the summer at a Catskills resort with her family, Frances "Baby" Houseman falls in love with the camp's dance instructor, Johnny Castle.

☐ **Funny Girl (1968)**
Starring: Barbra Streisand and Omar Sharif
Plot: The life of Fanny Brice, famed comedienne and entertainer of the early 1900s. We see her rise to fame as a Ziegfeld girl, subsequent career, and her personal life

☐ **Gentlemen Prefer Blondes (1953)**
Starring: Jane Russell and Marilyn Monroe
Plot: Showgirls Lorelei Lee and Dorothy Shaw travel to Paris, pursued by a private detective hired by the suspicious father of Lorelei's fiancé.

☐ **Gold Diggers of 1933 (1933)**
Starring: Warren William, Joan Blondell and Aline MacMahon
Plot: A wealthy composer rescues unemployed Broadway performers with a new play.

☐ **Grease (1978)**
Starring: John Travolta, Olivia Newton-John and Stockard Channing
Plot: Good girl Sandy and greaser Danny had fallen in love over the summer. When they discover they're now in the same high school, will they be able to rekindle their romance?

☐ **High Society (1956)**
Starring: Bing Crosby, Grace Kelly and Frank Sinatra
Plot: A spoiled heiress must choose among three suitors: her jazz musician ex-husband, a stuffy businessman and an undercover tabloid reporter.

☐ **A Star is Born (1954)**
Starring: Judy Garland and James Mason
Plot: A film star helps a young singer and actress find fame, even as age and alcoholism send his own career on a downward spiral.

More Movies to Watch

Dating... Mating... and Procreating

Oh, She's Fierce

This section is all about you being a fun, fearless female. You are feroosh. You can do anything you want; you are confident, you are the woman you have always aspired to be. You love doing things every single woman has wanted to do, and you go out and do them. You love life and you love the journey. Stop playing the games on Facebook of how many things you have done and go out and do them with class, sass, and a little bit of ass.

Why I get to continue to challenge myself, I...

_____
_____
_____
_____

- ☐ Date three men at once
- ☐ Have a one-night stand
- ☐ Threesome
- ☐ Orgy maybe?
- ☐ Go on a double date
- ☐ Go on a blind date
- ☐ Go on at least one date a week with a different person.
- ☐ Take cute polaroids on a date
- ☐ Go on a beach picnic
- ☐ Bonfire on the beach
- ☐ Share an ice cream cone on a date
- ☐ Have sex on the first date
- ☐ Ask each person you go out with to recreate one viral meme with you
- ☐ Use a dating app while you're on vacation and actually meet up with them. They might know cool spots you are unaware of.
- ☐ Buy matching swimwear with your date for a day
- ☐ Play truth or dare on a first date
- ☐ Host a singles-only party. Things you'll need: chips and guac, alcohol, name tags, and a piñata filled with condoms, dental dams and low-budget sex toys
- ☐ Have a one-night stand with a stranger in a new city
- ☐ Join the mile-high club
- ☐ Split a plate of spaghetti Lady-and-the-Tramp-style

- ☐ Show up to a date in a trench coat with nothing underneath
- ☐ Pretend to be a couple and get a psychic reading on the first date
- ☐ Go on a date with someone who is the opposite of your type
- ☐ Wink at someone across the room
- ☐ Tell a guy he's hot

- ☐ Go speed dating
- ☐ Ask a stranger to pretend to propose to you at a dive bar to try to get a free round of drinks.
- ☐ Skinny dip
- ☐ Let someone feed you peeled, seedless grapes

Other Single things I need to do...

- ☐ _____
- ☐ _____
- ☐ _____
- ☐ _____
- ☐ _____
- ☐ _____
- ☐ _____
- ☐ _____
- ☐ _____
- ☐ _____
- ☐ _____
- ☐ _____
- ☐ _____
- ☐ _____
- ☐ _____
- ☐ _____
- ☐ _____
- ☐ _____
- ☐ _____
- ☐ _____
- ☐ _____
- ☐ _____
- ☐ _____
- ☐ _____

- ☐ _____
- ☐ _____
- ☐ _____
- ☐ _____
- ☐ _____
- ☐ _____
- ☐ _____
- ☐ _____
- ☐ _____
- ☐ _____
- ☐ _____
- ☐ _____
- ☐ _____
- ☐ _____
- ☐ _____
- ☐ _____
- ☐ _____
- ☐ _____
- ☐ _____
- ☐ _____
- ☐ _____
- ☐ _____
- ☐ _____
- ☐ _____

My Favorite Memory
_____
_____
_____
_____
_____
_____

My Favorite Memory
_____
_____
_____
_____
_____
_____

My Favorite Memory
_____
_____
_____
_____
_____
_____

The Lessons I Have Learned
_____
_____
_____
_____
_____
_____

The Lessons I Have Learned
_____
_____
_____
_____
_____
_____

EXPERIMENTAL DATING IDEAS

In this day and age, everyone is always on their phones checking social media. No one knows each other anymore. We do online dating, then we go out for a drink to get to know the people we meet online, only to have the most miserable time and continuously want to check our newsfeeds. Instead of always going out for a standard drink or dinner, I suggest trying a few of these instead. I put this list together, to motivate you to get out and start having fun. Don't waste your life checking your stupid phone. Go out and live your life!

- ☐ **Write your own poems.** Read classic poems or even song lyrics to your beloved.
- ☐ **Read each other's Tarot cards.** Go to a psychic. Or go get your palms read.
- ☐ **Play board games.** At a coffee shop, or play billiard games at a bar.
- ☐ **Go thrift shopping.**
- ☐ **Stay at a sleazy hotel.** Have some cheap, raunchy fun.
- ☐ **Dance party for two.** Stay at home and dance with alcohol in hand and, of course, 80s tunes playing. I love dancing to "Running on a dream." Or the iconic dance in *The Breakfast Club*.
- ☐ **Draw each other naked.** (Obviously not on a first date… or maybe…)
- ☐ **Play "Photo Shoot".** Do a Boudoir shoot. Pretend a doll is a full-size person. Make huge things look small, or small things look big. Mimic iconic photos. #ChallengeAccepted
- ☐ **Make desserts together.** Cupcakes, cookies, you name it.
- ☐ **Indulge in a Tour de Food.** This is where you order one very small item from as many restaurants as possible until you are full.
- ☐ **Take a painting class together.**
- ☐ **Watch Lifetime movies.** Or really bad cult movies.
- ☐ **Go to an arcade.**
- ☐ **Sing karaoke but figure out a way to make it interesting.** Take the book and flip to a random page and pick the first song. Whatever you want to do. Be creative.
- ☐ **Sign up for Groupon and buy the first offer they have.** (If it isn't too expensive.) Make that your mandatory first date- no matter how silly it is.
- ☐ **Make astrology charts.**

- [ ] **Go to SnoCross.** (This might be just a Wisconsin thing).
- [ ] **Go tubing/water skiing/wakeboarding/pontooning.**
- [ ] **Throw a themed party.** Halo, International Food, Everybody's Birthday, Throw Back Thursday, Chili Cook-Off, Hannah Montana, etc.
- [ ] **At home food challenge.** Without going to the grocery store, try as hard as you can to create a meal using the ingredients in your cupboard.
- [ ] **Monster truck rally.**
- [ ] **Be a tourist.** Think of the absolute most tourist-y thing you could do in your city. If you can't think of it then go to a "Visit (enter your city name here)" website, choose one and go do it.
- [ ] **Watch shooting stars.** Figure out when the next comet shower is and plan on camping out to see it.
- [ ] **Get drunk while wearing formal attire at home.**
- [ ] **Bring half an evening.** One person organizes the food and the other organizes a movie viewing, or one person organizes tickets to an amusement park and the other plans a walking tour. Very collaborative!
- [ ] **The double-Netflix date.** You pick one. They pick one. Or a movie marathon and pick a theme. Brings a whole new term to Netflix and Chill.
- [ ] **The Case of The Mystery Band.** Grab a copy of your local newspaper or magazine, close your eyes, run your finger over the "live music" section & choose a band neither of you have ever heard of to go see.
- [ ] **Make a fort.**
- [ ] **Bring your favorite book & read the first chapter aloud.**
- [ ] **Random restaurant date.** Search Yelp for restaurants in your area, close your eyes, scroll and point at the screen.
- [ ] **Decorate a Christmas tree together.** Also kiss under the mistletoe and go ice skating. Decorate sugar cookies and make a gingerbread house. Or if that is too much because you aren't that serious, drive around neighborhoods looking at Christmas lights.
- [ ] **The Sunday New York Times crossword date.**
- [ ] **Playground date.** Slides are exciting. Monkey bars are fun. Swinging side by side is totally awesome.
- [ ] **Tree-climbing date.** You can also make a tree fort.
- [ ] **The photobooth hunt.** Troll your city for old-school photobooths and take as many strips as you can. Bring props and see how bizarre you can make them. Photobooth.net is your go-to source for major cities' photobooth info!

- ☐ **"My old neighborhood" date.** Walk around the area you used to live in (if it's accessible) and tell your date about all the crazy stories and mishaps you got into. Walk around to different bars and tell stories about what happened in them. This could be embarrassing, but so fun.

- ☐ **Go listen to a jazz concert, maybe in the park.**

- ☐ **Take cameras & explore an abandoned place.**

- ☐ **Medieval Times.** Google that shit, they are everywhere.

- ☐ **"First date" night.** For example, if you've been together for 3 years & live in the same house. Get dressed separately, meet somewhere strange & a bit awkward, & pretend you don't know one another. Start from scratch. Ask all those banal questions you're supposed to ask.

- ☐ **The generational date.** Pretend you're an age that you're not, then act accordingly. A senior citizens date might involve going lawn bowling, making apple sauce & watching The Price Is Right. A teenager date might involve roller-skating, making out in public and drinking vodka in an alleyway.

- ☐ **The recession date.** Do the Triple B's: eat at Burger King, take the bus to get there, then go play bingo. Maybe you could go window shopping afterwards.

- ☐ **The silent date.** In a loud, noisy, overstimulating world, it can be nice to unplug escape. Hold hands. Mime everything and most importantly no phones!

- ☐ **Make a video & put it on YouTube.**

- ☐ **Live feed your date.** Upload pictures, even give it a hashtag. This is probably not ideal for your first few dates with someone. Wait until you know each other a little better.

- ☐ **Travel without going anywhere.** The premise is simple. Have a normal date but speak with an accent. You both have to do it.

- ☐ **Write letters to each other.** Maybe love letters? Or funny letters? The sky is the limit. Be creative.

- ☐ **Dye each other's hair.** Crazy Colors are in right now, so go wild.

- ☐ **Sneak into a rooftop pool.**

- ☐ **Jump on a trampoline.** Or got to a trampoline gym where they have those fun obstacle courses.

- ☐ **Use sparklers to draw each other pictures.**

- ☐ **Have a Murder Mystery Dinner.**

- ☐ **Ice cream parlor.** Get a really, really, really big sundae and split it.

- ☐ **Have a five-course dinner that spans different restaurants.** Have an appetizer at one place, soup somewhere else, a main at another, a dessert at a place best known for their desserts.

- ☐ **Three-hour make-out session.**

☐ **Make up a dance together.**

☐ **Axe throwing.**

☐ **Do DIY wine tasting.** Have each person bring their two favorite types of wine, meet at a park, and pretend to write the description on the back of wine bottles when you try each type. Not a wino? Try it with beer, champagne, whiskey, vodka whatever you would like.

☐ **Go to a food festival or street fair.** The more adventurous and unique, the better.

☐ **Go on a scavenger hunt.** Make a list of a few things you've been dying to try and head out to find and experience them all. You can make it as simple or complicated as desired.

☐ **Choose your own adventure.** Pick a few favorite sites and activities, print out some pictures of them, choose a meeting place and let your date choose the adventure!

☐ **Make homemade pizza.**

☐ **Go to Chuck-E-Cheese.** Or Dave & Buster's.

☐ **Go to a Carnival.** Try all the carnival games and see if you can win a stuffed animal.

☐ **Paint each other's faces and go walk around in public.**

☐ **Go to a comedy club.**

☐ **Play games in the park.** Pack a picnic, your UNO cards, and a blanket.

☐ **Play at target.** Head over to Target (or any other retail store) later in the evening. Play with the toys, peruse the books, and even play hide-and-seek.

☐ **Play night games.** Try Ghosts in the Graveyard or Capture the Flag at night.

☐ **Escape rooms.** There are fun ones and there are scary ones. Test your problem-solving skills on these mini adventures. Pro tip: Don't go when you are hungry, you could be in there awhile.

☐ **See the *Rocky Horror Picture Show*.** Dress up as one of your favorite characters and act it out with the other moviegoers at a Halloween screening.

OTHER EXPERIMENTAL DATING IDEAS

☐ _____
☐ _____
☐ _____
☐ _____
☐ _____
☐ _____
☐ _____
☐ _____
☐ _____
☐ _____
☐ _____
☐ _____
☐ _____
☐ _____
☐ _____
☐ _____
☐ _____
☐ _____
☐ _____
☐ _____
☐ _____
☐ _____
☐ _____
☐ _____
☐ _____
☐ _____
☐ _____
☐ _____
☐ _____
☐ _____

☐ _____
☐ _____
☐ _____
☐ _____
☐ _____
☐ _____
☐ _____
☐ _____
☐ _____
☐ _____
☐ _____
☐ _____
☐ _____
☐ _____
☐ _____
☐ _____
☐ _____
☐ _____
☐ _____
☐ _____
☐ _____
☐ _____
☐ _____
☐ _____
☐ _____
☐ _____
☐ _____
☐ _____
☐ _____
☐ _____

EXPERIENCE ALL 30 KISSING TECHNIQUES

We have all experienced them. The terrible kissers. The sloppy, slobbery, mouth-engulfing spitters. There are men who, right when they kiss you, make you want to drop your panties instantly so you can see what they can do down below. When you find a man, who knows what he's doing with his mouth, it feels like winning the lottery.

Now imagine that *you're* the one who's the bad kisser, but didn't know because no one ever told you. Even if you're not terrible, it never hurts to improve and learn some sexy new techniques.

I started getting curious about how a person could enhance their make-out game, and that's what led me to the Kama Sutra. I learned there are thirty different kissing techniques taught in the Kama Sutra, and I can't wait to try out each and every one on some lucky guy. Of course, you need to experience them all in your bucket list! Duh!

- ☐ **Askew kiss.** *When the heads of the two are tilted in opposite directions and then the two kiss. Heads bowed allow better contact of the lips and a deep penetration of the tongues.*

- ☐ **Bent kiss.** *When one of the two throws their head back and the other holds their head over their chin and kisses them. The sweetness and affection are the main emotions that are transmitted with this kiss. A kiss of this kind is appropriate for the early stages.*

- ☐ **Direct kiss.** *When the lips of both bind directly and suck as if it were a ripe fruit. It is a kind of kiss where what matters are the lips sucking, nibbling and caressing gently with the tongue.*

- ☐ **Kiss pressure.** *The lips are pressed tightly with your mouth closed. A kiss to start or to end the relationship, should not keep for long. The teeth are stuck on the inside of the mouth and can leave blood.*

- ☐ **Top kiss.** *When the man initiates the kissing by getting the upper lip of the woman while the woman gets his lower lip and they share a beautiful kiss utilizing the whole of each other's lips. In the description of this kiss, it says that one takes the initiative and the other is limited to respond, possibly because the Kama Sutra was written for an active partner and a passive partner. I think that you can interpret these kisses any way you want. Don't limit yourself to the playing just the passive role, unless you enjoy that.*

- ☐ **Kiss clip.** *When the tongue touches the teeth, gums, tongue or palate of the other, called "Fight of the Tongue." In my opinion, this sounds sloppy.*

- ☐ **Throbbing kiss.** *This is nothing but a consequence of the slight opening up on the woman's part so that she feels the desire to touch the mouth that is kissing her, with her lips and so she moves her lower lip only.*

- ☐ **Contact kiss.** *When the tongue lightly touches the other's mouth and barely touches the partner's lips.*

- ☐ **Kiss to ignite.** *The flame is the kiss at the corners of the mouth that usually occurs in the middle of the night to kindle love, that looks innocent but may not be.*

- ☐ **Kiss to distract.** *When you want to draw your attention to your kisses. Remember that not all kisses have to be on the mouth! According to the Kama Sutra, other recommended places to start "the battle" are the forehead, eyes, cheeks, throat, chest, nipples, the area inside the mouth, hairline, neck and clavicle.*

- ☐ **Nominal kiss.** *When the woman doesn't really play a part in the kisses but merely allows her lover to make the move while only touching her lips to his.*

- ☐ **Kiss with your eyelashes.** *Touch and caress the other person's lips lightly with your eyelashes.*

- ☐ **Kiss with a finger.** *When the lover crosses the mouth of the beloved, inside and out with a finger.*

- ☐ **Kiss with two fingers.** *When the lover takes their fingers, wets them slightly and presses the mouth of the beloved.*

- ☐ **Kiss that awakens.** *The kiss that is given on the temples, near the hairline, while the other is asleep, to wake them gently.*

- ☐ **Public kiss.** *One of the two approaches the other and kisses him gently on the hand or neck.*

- ☐ **The kiss of remembrance.** *This is when the lovers are resting, satisfied with the passion, and one of them puts their head on the thigh of the other and drops, as if asleep, kissing them on the thigh or great toe.*

- ☐ **Transferred kiss.** *When the lover kisses a portrait, image or statue in the presence of the beloved, looking for the beloved to know that this kiss is for them.*

- ☐ **Tearful kiss.** *When one of the two longs so much for the other that in its absence, kisses their portrait and the partner can feel it.*

- ☐ **Kiss traveler.** *Although it seems kisses always tend to focus on the mouth, lips caressing other parts of the body is another exciting kissing technique.*

- ☐ **Kiss the breast.** *The most effective kisses on her nipples are first applied gently and with a little saliva. Then the pressure intensifies, and if the couple wants and likes, take the nipple with a little teeth and press gently. Some people prefer to feel some pain when they are about to have an orgasm.*

- ☐ **Kiss without a clock.** *The key is to pay full attention to each other's bodies. The more control you have and the more you concentrate on stroking and kissing every inch of the body, the stronger the feeling of pleasure are for both.*

- ☐ **Bite of the boar.** *The trail left on the skin is of many rows of sharp markings, very close to each other, and with red intervals as the tracks usually left by the pigs in the mud. It is a bite that is often on the shoulder.*

- ☐ **The stream tag.** *Consists of uneven skin surveys in a circle, produced by the spaces between teeth.* The Kama Sutra specifies that this type of bite should be on the chest.

- ☐ **Escondido bite.** *The bite that leaves a red mark and intended to be given on the lower lip.*

- ☐ **Bite classic.** *When taken between the teeth a lot of skin.*

- ☐ **The point.** *When taken between the teeth a small amount of skin so that the only mark left is a red dot.*

- ☐ **Dashed line.** *When a little piece of skin is bitten with all the teeth and they all leave their marks. Should be on the forehead or thigh.*

- ☐ **The coral and the jewel.** *This bite results from coupling the teeth and lips. The lips are coral and teeth are the jewel.*

- ☐ **Jewelry line.** *When biting down with all the teeth.*

SEX POSITIONS

There are thousands upon thousands of sex positions and maybe you will create your own and coin the term. I left you a few that are supposedly the best at giving you orgasms. I left you 20 fun positions to try. Remember it's all about the angles. Then the rest of the list you are going to have to go to https://sexpositions.club/positions to see the pictures to understand. Or if that is no longer a proper website Google the terms. Also, as with most sex positions, you could get injured so play safe my friends. I would also suggest going to the website and printing out the positions. There are pretty much in that order and they are constantly adding new ones. There are 480 positions so far.

- ☐ **Missionary.** According to sex experts, women get the most pleasure out of basic missionary sex. There's nothing fancy about it, but women said they loved the closeness and the intimacy of having their partner's weight on them.

- ☐ **Reverse Cowgirl.** In this position, the man is either lying down or in a sitting position, and the female straddles him backwards, facing his feet instead of his face. It's a key position that also allows easy access to the clitoris, this position is the one that is most likely to facilitate an orgasm because direct clitoral stimulation is easy to engage in.

- ☐ **Doggie Style.** A great position for the woman because it allows her to have optimal control. She is able to adjust her range of motion for an angle that feels best. He can likely stimulate her G-spot and have access to her clitoris with his hand, her hand or a toy.

- ☐ **Girl on Top.** Another position that allows her to have the most control of her orgasm is when she's the one on top, facing forward. When the woman is on top, she's in control of the depth and motion, as well as having easy access to her clitoris for pleasure.

- ☐ **Spooning.** It concentrates on stimulation of the front portion of the vagina or rectum, which is where the most nerves are located in the genitals.

- ☐ **Crisscross.** Both partners are lying down. The woman is on her back and the guy is on his side. She has her legs draped over his middle like a giant X. Since your bodies aren't squished against each other, reach down to rub the clitoris.

- ☐ **The Pillow Technique.** Positions often become more pleasurable for a woman when a pillow or blanket is added to create a new angle of entry. In missionary.

- ☐ **Ankles Up.** Put your ankles up over his shoulders. It allows him to go as deep inside as possible and hit the G-spot. The same deepness can also be achieved by you bending your knees or placing the soles of your feet on his chest.

TWENTY FUN SEX POSITIONS

☐ Amateur

☐ Cobra

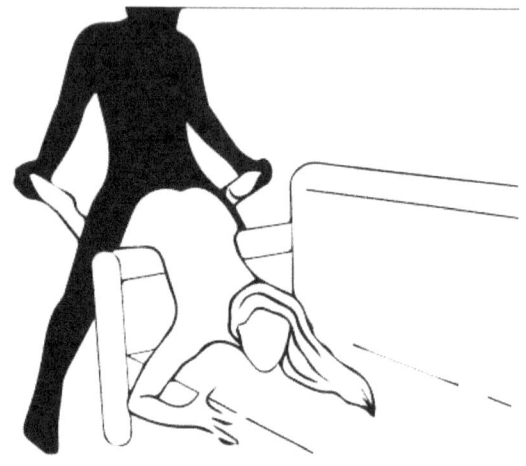

☐ Athlete

☐ Concubine

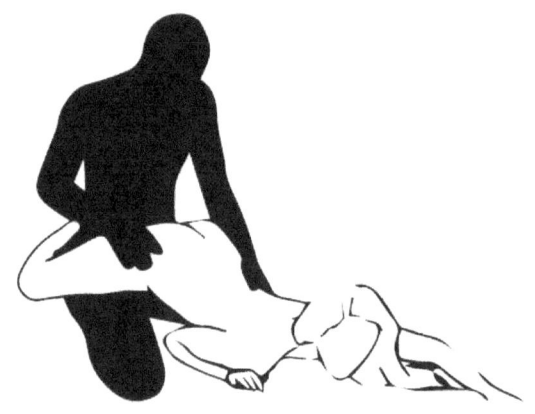

☐ Captivity

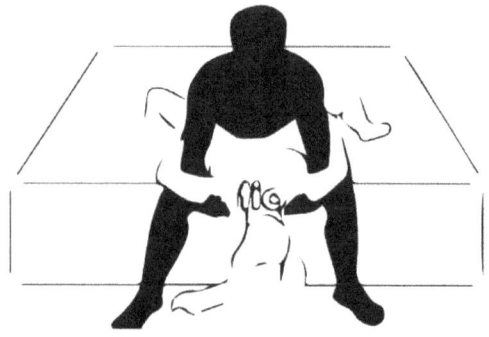

☐ Deck Chair

☐ Drowning Dog

☐ Eagle

☐ Intimate launch pad

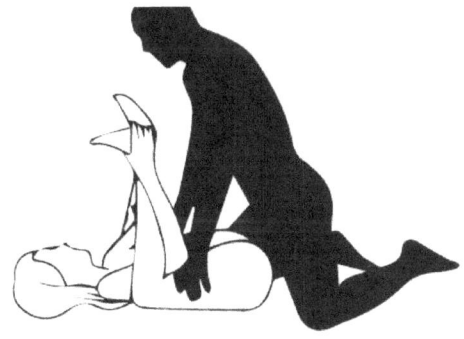

☐ Jack

☐ Low Doggy

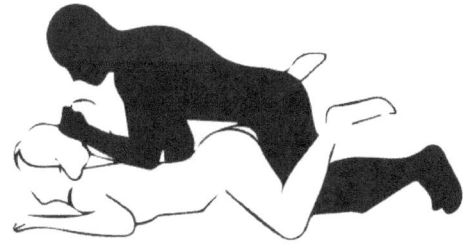

☐ Low start

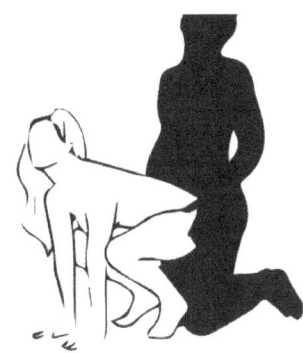

☐ Mature lady

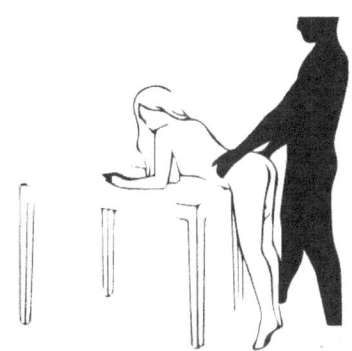

☐ Orgasmic penetration

☐ Penguin

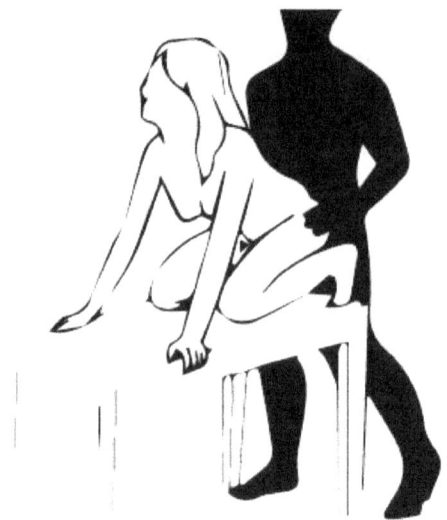

☐ Titanic-2

☐ Riverside

☐ Worship

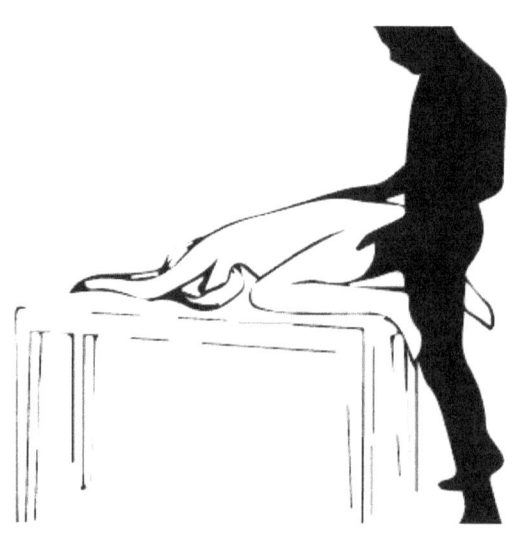

☐ Tight Vagina

☐ Wrestling

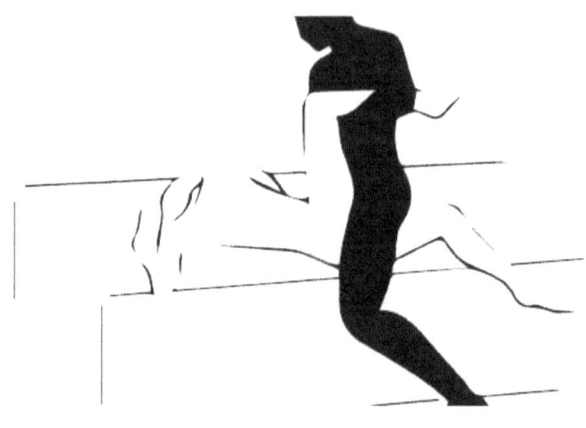

OTHER SEX POSITIONS I WANT TO TRY

☐ _____ ☐ _____
☐ _____ ☐ _____
☐ _____ ☐ _____
☐ _____ ☐ _____
☐ _____ ☐ _____
☐ _____ ☐ _____
☐ _____ ☐ _____
☐ _____ ☐ _____
☐ _____ ☐ _____
☐ _____ ☐ _____
☐ _____ ☐ _____
☐ _____ ☐ _____
☐ _____ ☐ _____
☐ _____ ☐ _____
☐ _____ ☐ _____
☐ _____ ☐ _____
☐ _____ ☐ _____
☐ _____ ☐ _____
☐ _____ ☐ _____
☐ _____ ☐ _____
☐ _____ ☐ _____
☐ _____ ☐ _____
☐ _____ ☐ _____
☐ _____ ☐ _____
☐ _____ ☐ _____
☐ _____ ☐ _____
☐ _____ ☐ _____
☐ _____ ☐ _____
☐ _____ ☐ _____
☐ _____ ☐ _____

EXPERIENCE ALL 11 ORGASMS

Did you know there are 11 different types of orgasms a woman can have????!!!! Yes, 11!!! Read about all of them and start checking them off your bucket list once you have achieved full glory.

- ☐ **Clitoral Orgasm.** You know the external sweet spot is highly sensitive, thanks to the 8,000 nerve endings that congregate there. And if you're like most women, it's the go-to point of stimulation to send you over the edge.

- ☐ **Vaginal Orgasm.** Though there is still some debate as to whether the G-spot exists, 30 percent of women claim they can have a big O from having the famous erogenous zone stimulated through penetration alone.

- ☐ **Blended Orgasm.** Experts say a combined clitoral and vaginal orgasm is the most powerful finale (it can be twice as strong and intense as either orgasm is by itself).

- ☐ **Multiple Orgasms.** To be clear, multiple orgasms happen one right after the next, not at different times in one session (although those are great too). Studies show that multiple orgasms are possible for some women if they can withstand being continuously stimulated after their first (and second and...) "finishes." (I did not know that's what it meant...I don't think most guys know this either)

- ☐ **The A-Spot Orgasm (The Anterior Fornix Orgasm).** This kind of female orgasm is achieved by stimulation of an area deep in the vagina (about 4-5 inches) on the front wall. It is the same wall where the G-Spot is situated. In other words, this is a patch of sensitive tissue at the inner front end of the vaginal tube, between the cervix and the bladder. After an orgasm, the A-Spot does not become too sensitive, and you can easily continue stimulation, bringing your partner to new heights of pleasure, this is why women are able to achieve multiple orgasms. Many women find the feeling incredibly pleasurable, while some may not like it at all. Keep this in mind when experimenting.

- ☐ **The Deep Spot Orgasm (The Posterior Fornix Orgasm).** This kind of female orgasm is achieved by stimulating the area located almost all the way back in the deepest part of the back wall of the vagina, just before the cervix. Direct stimulation of the Deep Spot can cause very intense orgasms. Some women may feel as if they are having anal sex. This particular area is not widely known, so very few women have ever experienced those sensations.

- ☐ **The U-Spot Orgasm.** This kind of female orgasm comes from the stimulation of a small area of sensitive erectile tissue located just above and on either side of the urethral opening. It is in the small area between the urethra and the vagina. If this region is gently caressed with the finger, the tongue, or the tip of the penis, there is a powerful erotic response, you stimulate this area the same way you treat the clitoris.

- ☐ **The Breast Orgasm.** This kind of female orgasm occurs during a peak of stimulation to the breasts. The nipples connect to nerves in the female genitals and many women feel a direct connection with their clitoris when their nipples are stimulated. Many women feel increased sexual excitement when their nipples are stimulated but not all of them can experience the breast orgasm. This depends very much on how sensitive their nipples are.

- ☐ **The Oral Orgasm.** This orgasm can be experienced by women who are very sensitive orally. The mouth plays a big role in the sexual nervous system. The mouth orgasm can take place during any sensual oral activity such as kissing, licking, sucking, or performing oral sex. Many women describe the excitement as beginning in their lips and then spreading from the mouth to the genitals and all over the body.

- ☐ **The Skin Orgasm.** This orgasm can be brought about by massaging certain areas of female body that are not directly connected to the sexual nervous system. Examples include orgasms experienced by many women during sensual massages.

- ☐ **The Mental Orgasm.** This kind of female orgasm can happen during visual and auditory stimulation. Examples of such stimulation are movies, videos, or sexual behavior exhibited in front of others. Women become so turned on that they can actually experience an orgasm from the excitement alone.

PLACES TO HAVE SEX

How adventurous are you in the sexual world? Or are you more shy and keep it in the bedroom? Regardless, this list is for everyone. You can even tweak it; I will let you. You can cross them off, if you know you will definitely never try having sex in a certain rundown space. Remember this is all about fun and experiencing what turns you on, so you can have complete and utter bliss.

- ☐ **On top of the kitchen table.**
- ☐ **In an open field during a heavy fog.**
- ☐ **On a warm car hood while parked on the side of the road** (if it's raining… bonus)
- ☐ **In a tent.**
- ☐ **In a jacuzzi.** Having sex in a pool or lake sounds hot, but it actually makes you more susceptible to UTIs and STDS—not to mention that chlorine can make condoms less effective. Plus dries out your natural lubricant.
- ☐ **In a public restroom.** (This could be grungy, so don't touch anything)
- ☐ **While parked after driving down an old country road.** Push back the seats (or hop into the backseat) and steam up those windows. Another option: Both of you can get in the driver's seat, slide it back, and straddle him while he grabs the steering wheel for extra leverage. (This really only works if the guy is like 5'8 and the woman is 5'2)
- ☐ **On a ship in the middle of the ocean.**
- ☐ **In the woods.**
- ☐ **In your backyard in a sleeping bag under the stars.**
- ☐ **On top of a mountain bluff.** Just before the sun begins to rise or set.
- ☐ **At the gym.** (This doesn't interest me, but I am not that adventurous.)
- ☐ **On a dock at night.**
- ☐ **At a crowded party down a dimly lit secluded hallway.**
- ☐ **On top of satin sheets on a huge bed.**
- ☐ **Sneak into a park after dark and make use of the picnic table.** (make sure to bring a blanket to avoid splinters.)
- ☐ **In a barn.**
- ☐ **In the back of a limo.**
- ☐ **On a motorcycle.**
- ☐ **In the back of a taxi.** (I think some good finger-banging will suffice)
- ☐ **A dark corner in a crowded bar.**
- ☐ **At a strip club.**
- ☐ **At a hole-in-the-wall motel.**
- ☐ **At a crowded football game underneath the bleachers.**
- ☐ **Inside the college library.**
- ☐ **On a fishing boat or canoe in the middle of a lake.**
- ☐ **On the 50-yard line at night.**

- ☐ Inside an old deserted house.
- ☐ At a rock concert.
- ☐ On a blanket at an outdoor concert at night.
- ☐ In the dressing room of a department store.
- ☐ On a trampoline. Bouncing up and down might be interesting.
- ☐ At a fruit orchard.
- ☐ Inside a lighthouse.
- ☐ At the Empire State Building.
- ☐ At the bottom of a canyon or gorge.
- ☐ Down a dark alleyway.
- ☐ At a Christmas tree farm.
- ☐ On a train in the middle of the night.
- ☐ In the middle of a hay field.
- ☐ At a haunted corn maze on Halloween.
- ☐ At a museum.
- ☐ At a vineyard.
- ☐ Under a gazebo.
- ☐ In the middle of the golf course.
- ☐ Late night at the ballpark.
- ☐ Inside a cave or under an overhang.
- ☐ In a hunting lodge.
- ☐ At the end of an old dead-end country road.
- ☐ By a creek during the daytime.
- ☐ On your front or back porch in the early morning.
- ☐ On a 4-wheeler.
- ☐ At a pumpkin patch.
- ☐ On a tractor.
- ☐ In the back of an old school bus.
- ☐ At the train station.
- ☐ On a soft rug in front of a fireplace.
- ☐ At the automated car wash.
- ☐ On your porch swing.
- ☐ In a hammock.
- ☐ At a state park.
- ☐ On a screened-in porch during a storm.
- ☐ On a rooftop.
- ☐ On the Ferris wheel at the fair. (I feel another finger-banging sesh will suffice, like Reese Witherspoon and Mark Wahlberg in *Fear*.)
- ☐ Inside a sauna.
- ☐ On the deck of a yacht.
- ☐ On your blanket at a firework show on the 4th of July.
- ☐ In your garage.
- ☐ On a secluded beach.
- ☐ On the tennis courts at night.
- ☐ On an air mattress in the back of the truck.
- ☐ On the beach by the ocean at night time.
- ☐ In a pile of leaves. I don't know if this is sanitary or if you would want leaves in your crotch, but hey it's up to you.
- ☐ In wet grass.
- ☐ In the city park in front of a fountain at night.
- ☐ In a stairwell.
- ☐ In a university classroom.
- ☐ On a university quad during a school break.
- ☐ In a planetarium.
- ☐ Underneath a state line sign.

- ☐ **At a scenic overlook off of the highway.**
- ☐ **In a locker room.**
- ☐ **On a lifeguard stand.**
- ☐ **On a boulder.**
- ☐ **In an RV.**
- ☐ **In an igloo.**
- ☐ **At Disneyland.** My girlfriend said for some reason, Disneyland always made her horny.
- ☐ **In a bouncy house.**
- ☐ **At a wedding.**
- ☐ **Backstage in an auditorium.**
- ☐ **In a historic mansion.**
- ☐ **Stopped at an intersection.** (This might be better suited for a blow job.)
- ☐ **Under a willow tree.**
- ☐ **In a steam room.**
- ☐ **Underneath an umbrella the next time you head over to the beach.**
- ☐ **On top of the washing machine, so you can feel the vibrations.**
- ☐ **On the balcony of a hotel room or apartment complex, so you have a gorgeous view.**
- ☐ **In the bathroom of your favorite bar.** Because you don't want to wait until you get home to jump on top of each other.
- ☐ **In the shower, while you soap up each other's bodies.**
- ☐ **In front of a webcam, so strangers can watch you.** If you do this, you better figure out a way to get paid.
- ☐ **On top of the kitchen counters.** Where you can experience all new angles.
- ☐ **Bent over the arm of the couch.** You can also stack up the cushions under your lower back. This makes it more likely that you'll reach an orgasm.
- ☐ **Against the windows, so your neighbors can see you.** (This one does seem a little risky, be careful of breaking the glass!)
- ☐ **On your desk at work.** You're on the clock while you're on his cock.
- ☐ **On the floor of your bedroom.** Where things will feel fun and fresh.
- ☐ **In front of a mirror.** I can't tell you how much I love this or why it turns me on so much.
- ☐ **Against a bookcase in the library.** Where you're forced to keep your voices down.
- ☐ **In your childhood bedroom.** Because the "past you" never got any action in there.
- ☐ **In the back of a movie theater.** Where it's too dark for anyone to see you.
- ☐ **Inside of a photo booth.** You'll have pictures of the occasion. (This is probably going to have to be a quick one.)
- ☐ **In an elevator.** Where someone could walk in on you at any moment. (Rev each other up first, because it will be a quick ride.)
- ☐ **In a dark foggy cemetery.**
- ☐ **Underneath a waterfall.** Because what's more romantic than that?
- ☐ **On a swing set.** They have sex swings for your home, but I think the real thing will be better and there's no possibility of the ceiling collapsing.
- ☐ **On a picnic blanket.**
- ☐ **In a bubble bath.**
- ☐ **On top of a pool table.** Because any flat surface will work.
- ☐ **At a hotel.** You definitely have to role play a few kinky scenes.
- ☐ **On the stairs.** Bend over a few steps up from him so your parts are aligned.

Other Places I Want to Have Sex

- [ ] _____
- [ ] _____
- [ ] _____
- [ ] _____
- [ ] _____
- [ ] _____
- [ ] _____
- [ ] _____
- [ ] _____
- [ ] _____
- [ ] _____
- [ ] _____
- [ ] _____
- [ ] _____
- [ ] _____
- [ ] _____
- [ ] _____
- [ ] _____
- [ ] _____
- [ ] _____
- [ ] _____
- [ ] _____
- [ ] _____
- [ ] _____
- [ ] _____
- [ ] _____
- [ ] _____
- [ ] _____

...And Everything In Between

The Absolute Must List

This is the list you should absolutely do before you die…maybe or just one that you can cross off your list. I wouldn't recommend sitting on a jury, I would try to get out of it as much as possible. But, hey, it may be a good experience to talk about. This is just fun shit so don't get discouraged, and as always you can cross shit off you don't like.

What it means to me to accomplish what I set out to be...

_____
_____
_____
_____
_____

- ☐ Adopt a pet
- ☐ Buy a house
- ☐ Graduate college
- ☐ Be a bridesmaid
- ☐ Get married
- ☐ Go on a picnic
- ☐ Get a passport
- ☐ Shoot a gun
- ☐ Ride a horse
- ☐ Milk a cow
- ☐ Sing karaoke
- ☐ Learn a musical instrument
- ☐ Go wine tasting
- ☐ Go to a sex store
- ☐ Invest in a vibrator
- ☐ Fall in love
- ☐ Get your heartbroken
- ☐ Drive a convertible with the top down and music blaring
- ☐ Sit on a jury
- ☐ See a lunar eclipse
- ☐ Sleep under the stars
- ☐ Create your family tree
- ☐ Go on a road trip
- ☐ Donate blood
- ☐ Fly first class
- ☐ Ride in a limo

The Life Moments I will Cherish...

- [ ] _____
- [ ] _____
- [ ] _____
- [ ] _____
- [ ] _____
- [ ] _____
- [ ] _____
- [ ] _____
- [ ] _____
- [ ] _____
- [ ] _____
- [ ] _____
- [ ] _____
- [ ] _____
- [ ] _____
- [ ] _____
- [ ] _____
- [ ] _____
- [ ] _____
- [ ] _____
- [ ] _____
- [ ] _____
- [ ] _____
- [ ] _____
- [ ] _____
- [ ] _____
- [ ] _____
- [ ] _____
- [ ] _____
- [ ] _____

- [ ] _____
- [ ] _____
- [ ] _____
- [ ] _____
- [ ] _____
- [ ] _____
- [ ] _____
- [ ] _____
- [ ] _____
- [ ] _____
- [ ] _____
- [ ] _____
- [ ] _____
- [ ] _____
- [ ] _____
- [ ] _____
- [ ] _____
- [ ] _____
- [ ] _____
- [ ] _____
- [ ] _____
- [ ] _____
- [ ] _____
- [ ] _____
- [ ] _____
- [ ] _____
- [ ] _____
- [ ] _____
- [ ] _____
- [ ] _____

My Favorite Memory

My Favorite Memory

My Favorite Memory

The Lessons I Have Learned

The Lessons I Have Learned

Learning Curve

What is life without learning something new? These are something things you probably learned when you were a kid, that made you smile when you finally figured out how to do it. These are things you may have always wanted to try but have never found the time to sit down and really concentrate. Whatever this list may be, think of it as a learning experience. See what I did there?

My favorite memory in school was...

_____
_____
_____
_____
_____

- ☐ Sew
- ☐ Braid hair
- ☐ Knit
- ☐ Water ski
- ☐ Snowboard
- ☐ Paddle board
- ☐ Scuba dive
- ☐ Surf

- ☐ Ride a bike
- ☐ Juggle
- ☐ Meditate
- ☐ Ice skate
- ☐ How to Speed read
- ☐ Fly a plane
- ☐ Speak another language

What else I want to learn...

- ☐ _____
- ☐ _____
- ☐ _____
- ☐ _____
- ☐ _____
- ☐ _____

- ☐ _____
- ☐ _____
- ☐ _____
- ☐ _____
- ☐ _____
- ☐ _____

My Favorite Memory

My Favorite Memory

My Favorite Memory

The Lessons I Have Learned

The Lessons I Have Learned

Classes

These classes can be anything and everything you have ever wanted to try. They can be online classes, workout classes, night classes, and whatever other classes I missed here. Have fun, this journey is all about learning what you like and don't like. If I have said it once, I've probably said it at least seven times in this book.

Why I love taking action and experiencing new things

_____
_____
_____
_____
_____

- ☐ Self-Defense
- ☐ Salsa lessons
- ☐ Cooking
- ☐ Photography
- ☐ Painting
- ☐ Sculpting
- ☐ A sexy hip-hop dance class
- ☐ Creative writing
- ☐ Auto mechanics. (Good to know so jerkoffs don't rip you off at the auto shop.)
- ☐ Take a psych or sociology class to study human behavior and interaction.

Other classes I want to take...

- ☐ _____
- ☐ _____
- ☐ _____
- ☐ _____
- ☐ _____
- ☐ _____
- ☐ _____
- ☐ _____
- ☐ _____
- ☐ _____
- ☐ _____
- ☐ _____

My Favorite Memory

My Favorite Memory

My Favorite Memory

The Lessons I Have Learned

The Lessons I Have Learned

Sporty Spice

This is all about your adventurous side. This section won't be for all of you, but is definitely for the tomboy inside. This is about your physical health mixed in with a little bit of mental health relaxation.

When I am active, I feel...

_____
_____
_____
_____
_____

- ☐ Parasailing
- ☐ Canoeing
- ☐ Rock climbing
- ☐ Ziplining
- ☐ Snorkeling
- ☐ Backflips
- ☐ Sailing
- ☐ Get a colonic
- ☐ Bikram yoga
- ☐ Pilates
- ☐ Zero gravity Pilates
- ☐ Pole dancing
- ☐ Spin class
- ☐ Zumba class
- ☐ Bar Method ballet workout
- ☐ Skydiving
- ☐ Hiking
- ☐ Bowling
- ☐ Join a volleyball or softball league
- ☐ Take a burlesque class
- ☐ Belly dancing
- ☐ Deep sea fishing
- ☐ Get a hole-in-one in golf
- ☐ Run a Tough Mudder obstacle race
- ☐ Compete in a triathlon
- ☐ Fast for 48 hours
- ☐ Bungee jump
- ☐ Jet ski
- ☐ Paragliding
- ☐ Goat yoga
- ☐ Run a marathon
- ☐ Take a flyboarding jetpack flight
- ☐ Rappel off a building

Other sporty things I need to do...

My Favorite Memory

My Favorite Memory

My Favorite Memory

The Lessons I Have Learned

The Lessons I Have Learned

Being a Kid Again

I don't care if you did these as a kid, you need to do these again. We get to let our inner child out sometimes. If we were unfortunate and didn't get to enjoy our childlike features, we get to experience them as adults. It is ok to be a kid again.

Why it's important to me to stay young at heart...

_____
_____
_____
_____
_____

- ☐ Make a snow angel
- ☐ Swing on a swing set
- ☐ Build a snowman
- ☐ Bury yourself in the sand
- ☐ Go sledding
- ☐ Roll down a hill
- ☐ Go to the batting cages
- ☐ Play miniature golf
- ☐ Ride every ride at an amusement park
- ☐ Laser tag
- ☐ Paintball
- ☐ Tell scary stories in a haunted house
- ☐ Join a choir or act in a play
- ☐ Write a fan letter to your all-time favorite hero or heroine
- ☐ Stay at a haunted house
- ☐ Write to a pen pal
- ☐ Spend the night in a treehouse

What else I cherish about acting like a kid again...

- ☐ _____
- ☐ _____
- ☐ _____
- ☐ _____
- ☐ _____
- ☐ _____
- ☐ _____
- ☐ _____
- ☐ _____
- ☐ _____

My Favorite Memory

My Favorite Memory

My Favorite Memory

The Lessons I Have Learned

The Lessons I Have Learned

Events

Have you ever watched your idol live? Were they everything you wanted and you swear they gazed into your eyes? Or tailgated at sporting venues meeting guys and drinking beers? This section is for you. Let's go be social and root for the single woman! As Nicole Arbour says "Go team!"

Why it's important to me to stay social...

_____
_____
_____
_____
_____

- ☐ The Super Bowl
- ☐ The Olympics
- ☐ The World Cup
- ☐ Your favorite sports teams' game.
- ☐ A comedy show
- ☐ An improv show
- ☐ The U.S. Open Tennis Championships
- ☐ Catch a ball in the stands of an MLB stadium
- ☐ See your favorite band live

Other events I want to attend...

☐ _____ ☐ _____
☐ _____ ☐ _____
☐ _____ ☐ _____
☐ _____ ☐ _____
☐ _____ ☐ _____
☐ _____ ☐ _____
☐ _____ ☐ _____
☐ _____ ☐ _____

My Favorite Memory

My Favorite Memory

My Favorite Memory

The Lessons I Have Learned

The Lessons I Have Learned

The Philanthropist

As a young girl growing up, I have always wanted to be a writer and inspire women to be the most amazing versions of themselves. I want every woman to know, we are not in competition with each other, but to support each other in our endeavors. The world is abundant. My biggest dream is to be able to give all women that sense of freedom and security. I want to start a non-profit and help victims of human trafficking rebuild their lives. What is your selfless dream?

I want to do my part to be a better...

_____
_____
_____
_____

- ☐ Do a charity walk
- ☐ Plant a tree
- ☐ Help out at an animal shelter. Fun fact: playing with animals lowers your blood pressure.
- ☐ Spend the afternoon at a homeless shelter feeding those in need
- ☐ Volunteer in a third world country
- ☐ Bring toys to the Children's Hospital
- ☐ Organize an annual charity fundraiser
- ☐ Become someone's mentor
- ☐ Donate money to charity
- ☐ Set up a non-profit
- ☐ Get passionate about a cause and spend time helping out
- ☐ Donate money and put your name on it: scholarship, park bench, etc.

Other philanthropic things I want to do...

- ☐ _____
- ☐ _____
- ☐ _____
- ☐ _____
- ☐ _____
- ☐ _____
- ☐ _____
- ☐ _____

My Favorite Memory
_____
_____
_____
_____
_____
_____

My Favorite Memory
_____
_____
_____
_____
_____
_____

My Favorite Memory
_____
_____
_____
_____
_____
_____

The Lessons I Have Learned
_____
_____
_____
_____
_____
_____

The Lessons I Have Learned
_____
_____
_____
_____
_____
_____

The Little Things

These are just the little moments you will cherish forever. The things that might be the easiest to accomplish or the hardest depending how you look at life. It's just going out every day and living your life to the fullest. Even if your life is mundane, pick something little that you have never done before. It could be something you think is stupid, but you will still laugh while you do it. Let's challenge ourselves every day.

The smallest gift I received that had the greatest impact was...

_____
_____
_____
_____
_____

- ☐ Get hypnotized
- ☐ Experience zero gravity
- ☐ Jump in a pool fully-clothed
- ☐ Name a star
- ☐ Take a picture every day for a year
- ☐ Meet someone famous
- ☐ Attend a murder mystery dinner
- ☐ Go to a drive-in movie
- ☐ Attend a masquerade ball
- ☐ Watch the sunrise
- ☐ Ride a bike where there are breathtaking views
- ☐ Go on a ferris wheel and take an epic selfie at the very top
- ☐ Tell the bartender, "Surprise me"
- ☐ Watch the best rated movie from the year you were born, and then the worst
- ☐ Go out without underwear
- ☐ Sing the absolute loudest you can in the shower
- ☐ Submit a video to Ellen
- ☐ Try to get on a game show
- ☐ Go to a museum
- ☐ Spend an ENTIRE DAY unplugged
- ☐ Find any free concert. Don't look at what music is playing, just go.
- ☐ Watch the sunrise and sunset in the same day.
- ☐ Have your portrait painted
- ☐ Be an extra in a movie or TV show
- ☐ Send a message in a bottle

☐ Bury a time capsule for someone to find years to come
☐ Go on a submarine ride

☐ Take part in an audience for a TV show
☐ Eat at a 5-star restaurant
☐ See a rocket launch

Other little things I need to do...

☐ _____
☐ _____
☐ _____
☐ _____
☐ _____
☐ _____
☐ _____
☐ _____
☐ _____
☐ _____
☐ _____
☐ _____
☐ _____
☐ _____
☐ _____
☐ _____
☐ _____
☐ _____
☐ _____
☐ _____
☐ _____
☐ _____
☐ _____
☐ _____
☐ _____
☐ _____
☐ _____

☐ _____
☐ _____
☐ _____
☐ _____
☐ _____
☐ _____
☐ _____
☐ _____
☐ _____
☐ _____
☐ _____
☐ _____
☐ _____
☐ _____
☐ _____
☐ _____
☐ _____
☐ _____
☐ _____
☐ _____
☐ _____
☐ _____
☐ _____
☐ _____
☐ _____
☐ _____
☐ _____

My Favorite Memory
_____
_____
_____
_____
_____
_____

My Favorite Memory
_____
_____
_____
_____
_____
_____

My Favorite Memory
_____
_____
_____
_____
_____
_____

The Lessons I Have Learned
_____
_____
_____
_____
_____
_____

The Lessons I Have Learned
_____
_____
_____
_____
_____
_____

Crazy Town

Do you want to get out of your comfort zone? Are you afraid of public speaking? Are you worried about what other people think of you? Well that all is going to change, and it is going to change now. It's time to get these negative voices out of your head and into the streets where they belong. The more you challenge yourself, the easier it becomes. Go wild! These are all the things you would never think about doing in public, but now you can. I am giving you permission.

When I do something spontaneous, I feel...

_____
_____
_____
_____
_____

- ☐ Get in a taxi and yell follow that car!
- ☐ Be in a flash mob
- ☐ Ask a street musician to play your favorite song and dance with a stranger
- ☐ Get dressed in something you'd never wear and go out. Let your crazy clothes give you a new identity for the night.
- ☐ Introduce yourself to people at a bar with an alias name and an alias life.
- ☐ Photobomb a group of strangers.
- ☐ Tell the barista at Starbucks your name is Beyoncé
- ☐ Buy a custom cake that says something embarrassing. Some suggestions: "Sorry, You're Pregnant." or "I Had Sex with Your Brother."
- ☐ Wear a costume to a non-costume party, Elle Woods style.
- ☐ Wear a fun wig out in public
- ☐ Dance on a table
- ☐ Grab some friends and do an ultimate Dare Night
- ☐ Ride a mechanical bull
- ☐ Make a complete and utter fool of yourself
- ☐ Arrive at an airport and take a random flight
- ☐ Stay out all night dancing, go to work and never have gone home
- ☐ Put your name down to be a passenger of the first tourist shuttle to the moon

Other crazy things I need to do...

My Favorite Memory

My Favorite Memory

My Favorite Memory

The Lessons I Have Learned

The Lessons I Have Learned

Animal Lover

When I was younger, I wanted to be a zoologist, until I found out it pays absolute crap. I wanted to train whales, until I watched *Free Willy*. I have always loved animals and their "who cares" attitude. I crave the unconditional love dog's give. I could give or take cats on any given Sunday. I think a panda is my spirit animal. My favorite mammal is the dolphin because they are the only other mammal that has sex for pleasure.

I want to be carefree like an animal because...

_____
_____
_____
_____
_____

- ☐ Swim with dolphins
- ☐ Ride an elephant
- ☐ Go whale watching
- ☐ Hold a koala
- ☐ Go to the zoo
- ☐ Hold a sloth
- ☐ Swim with sharks

Other animals I need to see...

- ☐ Shoebill
- ☐ Glass Frog
- ☐ Wombat
- ☐ Sun Bear
- ☐ Aye-Aye
- ☐ Okapi
- ☐ Markhor
- ☐ Myotonic goats
- ☐ Saiga antelope
- ☐ Long-wattled umbrella bird
- ☐ Fossa
- ☐ Penis snake
- ☐ Lowland streaked tenrec
- ☐ Marabou stork
- ☐ Sunda colugo
- ☐ Pink fairy armadillo
- ☐ Kinkajou
- ☐ De Brazza's monkey
- ☐ Jabiru
- ☐ Narwhal

- ☐ Coatimundi
- ☐ Pangolin
- ☐ Echidna
- ☐ Glaucus atlanticus
- ☐ Mandrill
- ☐ Chameleon
- ☐ Comodo dragon
- ☐ Flamingo
- ☐ Puffin
- ☐ Crocodile
- ☐ Giraffe
- ☐ Armadillo
- ☐ Toucan
- ☐ Anteater
- ☐ Red panda
- ☐ Panda
- ☐ Ostrich
- ☐ Great white shark
- ☐ Moose
- ☐ Tiger
- ☐ Lion
- ☐ Kangaroo
- ☐ Penguin
- ☐ Howler monkey

Other animal-y things I need to do...

- ☐ _____
- ☐ _____
- ☐ _____
- ☐ _____
- ☐ _____
- ☐ _____
- ☐ _____
- ☐ _____
- ☐ _____
- ☐ _____
- ☐ _____
- ☐ _____
- ☐ _____
- ☐ _____
- ☐ _____
- ☐ _____
- ☐ _____
- ☐ _____
- ☐ _____
- ☐ _____
- ☐ _____
- ☐ _____
- ☐ _____
- ☐ _____
- ☐ _____
- ☐ _____
- ☐ _____
- ☐ _____
- ☐ _____
- ☐ _____
- ☐ _____
- ☐ _____
- ☐ _____
- ☐ _____
- ☐ _____
- ☐ _____
- ☐ _____
- ☐ _____

My Favorite Memory

My Favorite Memory

My Favorite Memory

The Lessons I Have Learned

The Lessons I Have Learned

Adulting

You know when you were little and all you wanted to do was grow up? What the hell were we thinking? I am 36-years-old and still feel like a child. I don't do the dishes when I am supposed to, I hate making my bed, but now it's like I have to do it. There are great things about being an adult and that is we get to do whatever we want. We can sleep until noon; we can have mimosas at brunch. You know why? Because we are finally adults, so act accordingly.

When I do adulting things I feel...

_____
_____
_____
_____
_____

- ☐ Host a dinner party
- ☐ Travel for the weekend to see an old friend or family member
- ☐ Buy dinner for yourself at a street vendor and find a park bench to sit, eat, and people watch
- ☐ Rent a fancy car and go on a weekend trip somewhere new
- ☐ Spend a random night in the city and get a hotel. Order room service in a robe like a boss
- ☐ Take yourself out for a glass of champagne at a restaurant with a good view
- ☐ Take yourself out on a dinner date
- ☐ Throw a tea party
- ☐ Read a book in one day
- ☐ Quit your job. It feels so good to take a job and shove it.
- ☐ Sit at a bar by yourself and drink a martini. Cool.
- ☐ Tell a stranger they're beautiful
- ☐ Find a really hard recipe and attempt it
- ☐ Go to your local farmer's market
- ☐ Join a book club
- ☐ Grow a garden
- ☐ Throw a huge party and invite every one of your friends
- ☐ Get to know your neighbors

Other adulting things I need to do...

- [ ] _____
- [ ] _____
- [ ] _____
- [ ] _____
- [ ] _____
- [ ] _____
- [ ] _____
- [ ] _____
- [ ] _____
- [ ] _____
- [ ] _____
- [ ] _____
- [ ] _____
- [ ] _____
- [ ] _____
- [ ] _____
- [ ] _____
- [ ] _____
- [ ] _____
- [ ] _____
- [ ] _____
- [ ] _____
- [ ] _____
- [ ] _____
- [ ] _____
- [ ] _____
- [ ] _____
- [ ] _____
- [ ] _____
- [ ] _____

- [ ] _____
- [ ] _____
- [ ] _____
- [ ] _____
- [ ] _____
- [ ] _____
- [ ] _____
- [ ] _____
- [ ] _____
- [ ] _____
- [ ] _____
- [ ] _____
- [ ] _____
- [ ] _____
- [ ] _____
- [ ] _____
- [ ] _____
- [ ] _____
- [ ] _____
- [ ] _____
- [ ] _____
- [ ] _____
- [ ] _____
- [ ] _____
- [ ] _____
- [ ] _____
- [ ] _____
- [ ] _____
- [ ] _____
- [ ] _____

My Favorite Memory

My Favorite Memory

My Favorite Memory

The Lessons I Have Learned

The Lessons I Have Learned

Living a Legacy of Financial Abundance

Have you ever wanted to be a millionaire, but struggled as to how you are going to get there? Yeah, me too. This section is huge milestones in your life, whatever they may be that makes you feel accomplished. It is fun to have goals and work towards them. Always remember though, they don't happen overnight and every other cliché out there.

How I have lived my life in abundance is...
_____
_____
_____
_____
_____

- ☐ Be the boss
- ☐ Ask for a raise
- ☐ Write your will
- ☐ Create your own website
- ☐ Build a multimillion-dollar business empire or just start your own business
- ☐ Set up a passive income machine
- ☐ Become a millionaire

- ☐ Buy property abroad
- ☐ Design and build your own house
- ☐ Write a book
- ☐ Give a TED Talk
- ☐ Make history
- ☐ Design an app
- ☐ Compose and release a music album

Other legacy things I need to do...

- ☐ _____
- ☐ _____
- ☐ _____
- ☐ _____
- ☐ _____

- ☐ _____
- ☐ _____
- ☐ _____
- ☐ _____
- ☐ _____

My Favorite Memory

My Favorite Memory

My Favorite Memory

The Lessons I Have Learned

The Lessons I Have Learned

Beauty/Self-Care

This section is all about Self-care and relaxation. This is about you and how you can take care of your mental health. This is about aging gracefully and trying out new ways to make you feel beautiful inside and out. Get ready to have your confidence soar! Isn't it fun be a woman? I think so. I love being a woman, I even love my cellulite. (Doesn't mean I am not trying to get rid of it.)

What makes me feel beautiful is...

_____
_____
_____
_____
_____

- ☐ Get a facial
- ☐ Get laser hair removal
- ☐ Buy a pair of Louboutin's
- ☐ Buy at least one designer handbag
- ☐ Get a massage
- ☐ Get a mani-pedi
- ☐ Go to a Korean spa
- ☐ Make a home spa day: bubble bath, candles, facial mask and wine.
- ☐ Get a bikini wax
- ☐ Buy yourself flowers.
- ☐ Invest in a little black dress and sexy stilettos
- ☐ Get your teeth whitened
- ☐ Get a spray tan
- ☐ Try an infrared sauna or heat wrap.
- ☐ Dye your hair a daring color
- ☐ Learn to take a compliment
- ☐ Write down your personal mission statement
- ☐ Forgive your parents
- ☐ Overcome your fear of failure
- ☐ Accept yourself for who you are
- ☐ Reflect on your greatest weakness, and realize it's your greatest strength
- ☐ Attend a Tony Robbins event
- ☐ Attend a meditation course
- ☐ Don't drink alcohol for a year
- ☐ Keep a daily gratitude journal

Other Beauty/Self-Care things I need to do...

- [ ] _____
- [ ] _____
- [ ] _____
- [ ] _____
- [ ] _____
- [ ] _____
- [ ] _____
- [ ] _____
- [ ] _____
- [ ] _____
- [ ] _____
- [ ] _____
- [ ] _____
- [ ] _____
- [ ] _____
- [ ] _____
- [ ] _____
- [ ] _____
- [ ] _____
- [ ] _____
- [ ] _____
- [ ] _____
- [ ] _____
- [ ] _____
- [ ] _____
- [ ] _____
- [ ] _____
- [ ] _____
- [ ] _____
- [ ] _____
- [ ] _____
- [ ] _____
- [ ] _____
- [ ] _____
- [ ] _____
- [ ] _____
- [ ] _____
- [ ] _____
- [ ] _____
- [ ] _____
- [ ] _____
- [ ] _____
- [ ] _____
- [ ] _____
- [ ] _____
- [ ] _____
- [ ] _____
- [ ] _____
- [ ] _____
- [ ] _____
- [ ] _____
- [ ] _____
- [ ] _____
- [ ] _____

My Favorite Memory

My Favorite Memory

My Favorite Memory

The Lessons I Have Learned

The Lessons I Have Learned

Food, Booze, Wine & Dine

Foods to Try Before You Die

What is your favorite food? How did you find out it was your favorite food and when? My favorite food is Chicken and Dumplings, homemade by my mother. I am not sure why, but to this day I can't get enough, but it's only the way she makes it. I don't like it at restaurants, the dumplings are never as big. I always disliked avocados until I had avocado toast. Yes, I may be basic, but I do not care.

- ☐ Abalone
- ☐ Avocado
- ☐ Bagel and Lox
- ☐ Baba Ghanoush
- ☐ Baklava
- ☐ Barbecue ribs
- ☐ Bibimbap
- ☐ Biscuits and gravy
- ☐ Black pudding
- ☐ Black truffle
- ☐ Borscht
- ☐ Bread pudding
- ☐ Calamari
- ☐ Caprese
- ☐ Carp
- ☐ Caviar
- ☐ Ceviche
- ☐ Cheese fondue
- ☐ Chicken and waffles
- ☐ Chicken tikka masala
- ☐ Chile relleno
- ☐ Chitlins
- ☐ Churros
- ☐ Clam chowder
- ☐ Crab cakes
- ☐ Crickets
- ☐ Deep dish pizza
- ☐ Dim sum
- ☐ Dulce de leche
- ☐ Eel
- ☐ Escargot
- ☐ Eggs Benedict
- ☐ Empanadas
- ☐ Fettuccini Alfredo
- ☐ Fish and chips
- ☐ Fresh spring rolls
- ☐ Fried green tomatoes
- ☐ Fried plantains
- ☐ Frog legs
- ☐ Fugu
- ☐ Funnel cake
- ☐ Gazpacho
- ☐ Goat cheese
- ☐ Goulash
- ☐ Grilled cheese and tomato soup
- ☐ Gumbo
- ☐ Gyro
- ☐ Haggis
- ☐ Honeycomb
- ☐ Huevos rancheros
- ☐ Hummus
- ☐ Hush puppies
- ☐ Jerk chicken
- ☐ Key lime pie
- ☐ Kimchi
- ☐ Kitfo
- ☐ Kobe beef
- ☐ Lobster or lobster roll
- ☐ Moon pie
- ☐ Mopane worms
- ☐ Octopus
- ☐ Okra
- ☐ Pad Thai
- ☐ Paella
- ☐ Paneer
- ☐ Pastrami on rye
- ☐ Pavlova
- ☐ Peking duck
- ☐ Phaal

- ☐ Philly cheese steak
- ☐ Pho
- ☐ Pig ears
- ☐ Pineapple and cottage cheese
- ☐ Poke
- ☐ Polenta
- ☐ Potato dumpling
- ☐ Poutine
- ☐ Prickly pear
- ☐ Rabbit stew
- ☐ Raw oysters
- ☐ Sauerkraut
- ☐ Sea urchin
- ☐ S'more
- ☐ Soft shell crab
- ☐ Som tam
- ☐ Spaetzle
- ☐ Spam
- ☐ Surströmming
- ☐ Sweet potato fries
- ☐ Tamale
- ☐ Tofu
- ☐ Tom yum
- ☐ Umeboshi
- ☐ Venison
- ☐ Wasabi peas
- ☐ Zucchini flowers

Other Foods to Try Before You Die

- ☐ _____
- ☐ _____
- ☐ _____
- ☐ _____
- ☐ _____
- ☐ _____
- ☐ _____
- ☐ _____
- ☐ _____
- ☐ _____
- ☐ _____
- ☐ _____
- ☐ _____
- ☐ _____
- ☐ _____
- ☐ _____
- ☐ _____
- ☐ _____
- ☐ _____
- ☐ _____
- ☐ _____
- ☐ _____
- ☐ _____
- ☐ _____
- ☐ _____
- ☐ _____
- ☐ _____
- ☐ _____
- ☐ _____
- ☐ _____
- ☐ _____
- ☐ _____
- ☐ _____
- ☐ _____
- ☐ _____
- ☐ _____
- ☐ _____
- ☐ _____
- ☐ _____
- ☐ _____
- ☐ _____
- ☐ _____

Exotic Fruits to Try Before you Die

Have you ever gone to the grocery story and thought, huh? What the hell is that? Or thought I sick of the same old sweets or fruits, well then, this list is for you. If you have never thought that, then maybe this list isn't for you, but there are some pretty damn good-tasting fruits out there that are better than your average strawberry.

- ☐ **Cherimoya.** Mark Twain once called it "the most delicious fruit known to man." The taste is tropical, somewhere between a pineapple and a banana. Both the seeds and skin are toxic so it must be peeled. Health benefits for this fruit are that it is high in fiber, iron, potassium, vitamin C and B.

- ☐ **Sweetsop.** A round or heart-shaped fruit. Often eaten on its own, blended into juice or made into ice cream. A good source of potassium, magnesium, iron, riboflavin, vitamin B and C.

- ☐ **Jackfruit.** The largest tree growing fruit in the region between India and Malaysia. It has a mild fruity flavor. A great vegan substitute for pulled pork. It's so starchy it can often replace potato in dishes. A source of protein, vitamin A, fiber, copper, and manganese. The seeds are edible and nutritious.

- ☐ **Araza.** Native to the Amazon jungle, it is often too acidic to eat on its own and its tart flavor is more popular when blended to make juice, ice cream and smoothies. Some research shows its nutrients could prevent cancer and control blood pressure.

- ☐ **Spanish lime.** Grown throughout the Caribbean and parts of South America. It is called Spanish lime because they look like small unripe limes, about the size of a ping pong ball. The flavor is often described as a mix between lime and lychee.

- ☐ **African horned cucumber.** The distinctive spiky skin of the fruit is what gives it its name. The green flesh has a tart flavor with a jelly-like texture. It tastes like a mix of kiwi, cucumber, banana and citrus. High in vitamin A, E, fiber, zinc and minerals. Some swear it has anti-aging properties.

- ☐ **Durian.** Famous throughout Southeast Asia for its strong smell. Known as the king of fruits, the most common kind has a green exterior with a yellow interior and an almond custard flavor.

- ☐ **Ciruela.** In the cashew fruit family and about the size of a kiwi. It has a very sweet flesh when ripe and tastes similar to a nectarine with mango or citrus. Known to help digestion and acid reflux, amongst other ailments. It is high in fiber and vitamin C as well as other antioxidants.

- ☐ **Mangosteen.** A distinctive tree-growing purple fruit, the white creamy flesh is both tart and sweet. Its taste is between a peach and a tangerine. It has been used to treat tuberculosis and cancer. It is rich in vitamin B and C, fiber, iron, riboflavin and manganese.

- ☐ **Ackee.** You can tell when it's ripe because the fruit will split to reveal the seeds and flesh. It is important to eat it only when ripe as it can be toxic. It is treated as a vegetable and cooked in dishes. The taste is similar to hearts of palm.

- ☐ **Feijoa.** Growing on shrubs in South America, these small fruits have a sweet flavor similar to pineapples. The texture is gritty like a pear. The skin should be peeled, as it is bitter.

- ☐ **Snake Fruit.** Also known as salak, is a common street food snack where vendors peel the skin and serve in small plastic bags. Named for distinctive colorful scales on the skin that are also quite prickly. It has a sweet flavor that is slightly acidic.

- ☐ **Cupuacu.** These fruits are related to cocoa, and beneath the brown skin is a white creamy flesh that has been compared to a blend of chocolate and pineapple. It is sweet and tart at the same time, like pineapple and mango mixed with pear and banana. It's also used in body lotions.

- ☐ **Jabuticaba.** One of the more usual exotic fruits, it grows in clusters on bark. While the fruit has a purple grape-like skin, the inside has a white gelatinous flesh. Like grapes, this fruit is often eaten raw, preserved to make jam, or fermented to make wine or alcohol.

- ☐ **Naseberry.** Also known as sapodilla or chikoo, this fruit is actually a large berry. It softens significantly when ripe and has a malty, sweet flavor, with a small seed within. It looks more like a potato than a fruit or a berry. The spiced flavor similar to nutmeg, cinnamon and allspice.

- ☐ **Guava.** The taste varies depending on how ripe it is and what kind. Can be as sweet as a pear or tart like a grapefruit. Common in juices, hot sauces and candies.

- ☐ **Pomelo.** A citrus fruit sometimes called a Chinese grapefruit. It has a thick layer of pith that must be removed to reach the edible portion. They are large fruit that can weigh several pounds.

- ☐ **Passionfruit.** This exotic fruit is actually a very large berry that can either be purple or yellow. Also known as the maracuja or lilikoi, it is now cultivated around the world and used in everything from fruit juice to ice cream. The fruits are small with a gelatinous seedy center.

- ☐ **Mamey Sapote.** Beneath the unattractive brown skin of this large berry, the flesh softens as it ripens, and is usually orange or yellow. Mamey Sapote has a spiced flavor and sometimes compared to a sweet potato. Commonly eaten raw or used in smoothies, ice cream, jams and desserts.

- ☐ **Langsat.** These small fruits look like a small potato with a gel-like interior. The fruit's flesh tastes sweet with a tangy edge, similar to combining a grape and a grapefruit. If the fruit is not ripe, the individual pieces are quite sour and sometimes bitter.

- ☐ **Miracle fruit.** The reason this berry is called a miracle is that after having one you can eat an onion and it will taste like an apple. The miracle fruit actually has a mild, sweet flavor on its own with a hint of tang.

- ☐ **Lulo.** This citrus fruit is also known as a naranjilla and has a citrus tang similar to rhubarb mixed with lime. It is also turned into wine in Colombia and used for ice cream.

- ☐ **Monstera Deliciosa.** A large monstrously delicious fruit that can be an irritant before it ripens. However, once it fully ripens it has a taste similar to a pineapple. For this reason, it is referred to as the fruit salad plant.

- ☐ **Dragon Fruit.** A colorful red and green cactus fruit with white flesh spotted with tiny black seeds, similar in texture to a kiwifruit. While the appearance is dramatic, the flavor was surprisingly subtle.

- ☐ **Kiwano.** A beautiful and otherworldly-looking fruit that is native to Sub-Saharan Africa. The fruit has bright orange spiky skin filled with yellow and green seeds. The vibrant flesh tastes like lemony cucumber.

- ☐ **Korean Melon.** A small yellow melon with deep white stripes and white interior flesh with small, edible white seeds. The fruit tastes like a cross between a honeydew melon and a cucumber, with the crisp texture of a cucumber.

- ☐ **Loquat.** A small, pear-shaped orange fruit with large seeds. It tastes like a combination of peach and mango.

- ☐ **Longan.** A small round fruit with a translucent white flesh and a shiny black seed. Longan means "dragon's eye" in Chinese, and is named because it looks like an eyeball when shelled. Native to South Asia and is similar in appearance and texture to lychee.

- ☐ **Physalis.** A small orange berry that is sour and sweet. It's related to tomatoes and tomatillos and you can sometimes see it sold encased in a papery husk similar to a tomatillo.

- ☐ **Mulberry.** An elongated red berry that grows on a small bushy, tree. It's native to China and was historically grown as fruit for silkworm larvae.

- ☐ **Jujube.** A small oval and sweet red fruit that wrinkles and looks like a date when it's mature. Native to China, but now grown around the world.

- ☐ **Chom Chom.** Don't worry, chom choms won't hurt you with those spiky-looking hairs. This stunning fruit has a flavor and texture similar to lychee, with a soft and juicy pale interior. Easy to eat a bunch at a time, just peel away the thin outer layer to get to the good stuff inside.

- ☐ **Star fruit.** Worth eating just because it looks *exactly* like a star when sliced, and also happens to be tasty. With flavors reminiscent of citrus fruit and plums, you can pop the whole thing into your mouth: seeds, skin and all.

- ☐ **Persimmon.** Although it may look like a tomato, the flavor couldn't be more different. It's sweet and firm flesh is sure to please everyone. Simply slice it up and enjoy, or let the fruit ripen until it's soft and develops a deeper sweetness, almost reminiscent of dates.

- ☐ **Sapodilla.** Pretty blah on the outside but packs a sugary punch with its extremely sweet, sunset-colored interior. It has the flavor of a caramelized pear, which means it can basically be dessert if you're looking to brag and say you had fruit for dessert.

Other Exotic Fruits to Try

Exotic Vegetables to Try Before you Die

Have you ever been to the grocery store and thought, man what the hell is that? Just kidding, but for real though, these veggies might help with your cooking. I suck at cooking and that is one skill I would like to master. I think knowing all the different type of vegetables you can cook with might help.

- ☐ Black radish
- ☐ Okinawan purple sweet Potato
- ☐ Chinese artichokes
- ☐ Fiddleheads
- ☐ Ramps
- ☐ Dulse
- ☐ Jicama
- ☐ Kohlrabi
- ☐ Romanesco broccoli
- ☐ Salsify
- ☐ Samphire
- ☐ Sunchoke
- ☐ Tomatillo
- ☐ White asparagus
- ☐ Oca
- ☐ Tiger nut
- ☐ Celeriac
- ☐ Kai Lan
- ☐ Nopal
- ☐ Manioc
- ☐ Apollo broccoli AKA broccolini
- ☐ Dragon carrot
- ☐ Red perilla (Shiso)
- ☐ Chinese flowering leek
- ☐ Winter squash
- ☐ Winter melon
- ☐ Wax gourd
- ☐ Chinese water spinach
- ☐ Lotus root
- ☐ Bitter melon
- ☐ Silk squash
- ☐ Bamboo shoot
- ☐ Saltwort
- ☐ Daikon radish
- ☐ Calabash AKA bottle gourd
- ☐ Yardlong beans
- ☐ Karela
- ☐ Garlic scapes
- ☐ Wan shen
- ☐ Cassava
- ☐ Malabar spinach
- ☐ Peter pepper
- ☐ Hen of the Woods
- ☐ Watercress
- ☐ Daikon
- ☐ Escarole

Other Exotic Vegetables to Try

- [ ] _____
- [ ] _____
- [ ] _____
- [ ] _____
- [ ] _____
- [ ] _____
- [ ] _____
- [ ] _____
- [ ] _____
- [ ] _____
- [ ] _____
- [ ] _____
- [ ] _____
- [ ] _____
- [ ] _____
- [ ] _____
- [ ] _____
- [ ] _____
- [ ] _____
- [ ] _____
- [ ] _____
- [ ] _____
- [ ] _____
- [ ] _____
- [ ] _____
- [ ] _____
- [ ] _____
- [ ] _____

- [ ] _____
- [ ] _____
- [ ] _____
- [ ] _____
- [ ] _____
- [ ] _____
- [ ] _____
- [ ] _____
- [ ] _____
- [ ] _____
- [ ] _____
- [ ] _____
- [ ] _____
- [ ] _____
- [ ] _____
- [ ] _____
- [ ] _____
- [ ] _____
- [ ] _____
- [ ] _____
- [ ] _____
- [ ] _____
- [ ] _____
- [ ] _____
- [ ] _____
- [ ] _____
- [ ] _____
- [ ] _____

Cocktails to try before you die

I recommend this list to conquer when you are in your twenties, because in your thirties you will have hangovers that last at least two days. Trust me. I am not an advocate of binge drinking, we are ladies, we need to keep up our glorified appearances. I know it happens. I've been there, and it was not pretty.

- ☐ Adios Mother F*cker
- ☐ Alabama Slammer
- ☐ Amaretto Sour
- ☐ Americano
- ☐ Aperol Spritz
- ☐ Apple Jacks
- ☐ Bahama Mama
- ☐ Bay Breeze
- ☐ Bellini
- ☐ Black'n'Tan
- ☐ Bloody Mary
- ☐ Blow Job
- ☐ Buttery Nipple
- ☐ Captain and Coke
- ☐ Cement Mixer
- ☐ Champagne
- ☐ Cosmopolitan
- ☐ Creamsicle
- ☐ Daiquiri
- ☐ Dirty Martini
- ☐ Eggnog
- ☐ Fuzzy Navel
- ☐ Gimlet
- ☐ Gin and Tonic
- ☐ Grasshopper
- ☐ Harvey Wallbanger
- ☐ Horny Bull
- ☐ Hot Toddy
- ☐ Hurricane
- ☐ Irish Car Bomb
- ☐ Irish Coffee
- ☐ Jell-O Shot
- ☐ Lemon Drop
- ☐ Mai Tai
- ☐ Manhattan
- ☐ Margarita
- ☐ Martini
- ☐ Miami Vice
- ☐ Midori Sour
- ☐ Mimosa
- ☐ Mojito
- ☐ Moscow Mule
- ☐ Mudslide
- ☐ Old Fashioned
- ☐ Pina Colada
- ☐ Red-Headed Slut
- ☐ Screwdriver
- ☐ Sea Breeze
- ☐ Seven and Seven
- ☐ Sex on the Beach
- ☐ Tequila Rose and Mountain Dew
- ☐ Tequila Sunrise
- ☐ Tom Collins
- ☐ Washington Apple
- ☐ Whiskey Straight
- ☐ White Russian

Other Cocktails to Try Before You Die

All the Wine in the World

These wine descriptions are from wines.com. How many have you heard of, and how many are excited to try? Anything and everything with wine is my motto. I love wine. Wine, wine, wine. My website has wine stains on it. I am obsessed with wine. Wine all the time. Cheers!

- ☐ **Albariño.** Spanish white wine grape that makes crisp, refreshing and light-bodied wines.
- ☐ **Aligoté.** White wine grape grown in Burgundy making medium-bodied, crisp, dry wines with spicy character.
- ☐ **Amarone.** From Italy's Veneto Region a strong, dry, long-lived red, made from a blend of partially dried red grapes.
- ☐ **Arneis.** A light-bodied dry wine the Piedmont Region of Italy
- ☐ **Asti Spumante.** From the Piedmont Region of Italy, a semidry sparkling wine produced from the Moscato di Canelli grape in the village of Asti.
- ☐ **Auslese.** German white wine from grapes that are very ripe and thus high in sugar.
- ☐ **Banylus.** A French wine made from late-harvest Grenache grapes and served with chocolate or dishes with a hint of sweetness. By law the wine must contain 15 percent alcohol.
- ☐ **Barbaresco.** A red wine from the Piedmont Region of Italy, made from Nebbiolo grapes it is lighter than Barolo.
- ☐ **Bardolino.** A light red wine from the Veneto Region of Italy. Blended from several grapes the wine garnet in color, dry and slightly bitter, sometimes lightly sparkling.
- ☐ **Barolo.** Highly regarded Italian red, made from Nebbiolo grapes. It is dark, full-bodied and high in tannin and alcohol. Ages well.
- ☐ **Beaujolais.** A light, fresh, fruity red wines from south of Burgundy, in eastern France.
- ☐ **Blanc de Blancs.** Champagne or white wine made from white grapes.
- ☐ **Blanc de Noirs.** White or blush wine or Champagne made from dark grapes.
- ☐ **Boal or Bual.** Grown on the island of Madeira, it makes medium-sweet wines.
- ☐ **Brunello.** This strain of Sangiovese is the only grape permitted for Brunello di Montalcino, the rare, costly Tuscan red. Luscious black and red fruits with chewy tannins.

- ☐ **Cabernet Franc.** It is an earlier-maturing red wine, due to its lower level of tannins. Light- to medium-bodied wine with more immediate fruit than Cabernet Sauvignon and some of the herbaceous odors evident in unripe Cabernet Sauvignon.

- ☐ **Cabernet Sauvignon.** Currant, plum, black cherry & spice, with notes of olive, vanilla mint, tobacco, toasty cedar, anise, pepper & herbs. Cabernet spends from 15 to 30 months aging in oak barrels which tend to soften the tannins, adding the toasty cedar & vanilla flavors.

- ☐ **Carignan.** Known as Carignane in California, and Sarnano in Italy. Once a major blending grape for jug wines, Carignan's popularity has diminished though it still appears in some blends.

- ☐ **Cava.** Spanish sparkling wine. Produced by the méthode champenoise.

- ☐ **Charbono.** Mainly found in California (may possibly be Dolcetto), this grape has dwindled in acreage. Often lean and tannic.

- ☐ **Champagne.** Ranges from burnt, caramelly oxidized to full bodied fruit and yeast characters to light and citrusy, and everything in between. Each of these wines can be altered in its amount of residual sweetness from a bone-chilling dryness to sugar syrup.

- ☐ **Chardonnay.** Apple, pear, vanilla, fig, peach, pineapple, melon, citrus, lemon, grapefruit, honey, spice, butterscotch, butter & hazelnut. Takes well to oak aging & barrel fermentation. Easy to manipulate with techniques like sur lie aging & malolactic fermentation.

- ☐ **Châteauneuf-du-Pape.** Most famous wine of the southern Rhône Valley. The reds are rich, ripe, and heady, with chewy rustic flavors. Although 13 grape varieties are planted here, the principal varietal is Grenache, followed by Syrah, Cinsault and Mourvèdre.

- ☐ **Chenin Blanc.** Native of the Loire where it's the basis of the famous whites: Vouvray, Anjou, Quarts de Chaume and Saumer. Called Steen in South Africa. It can be a pleasant wine, with melon, peach, spice and citrus. Depending on the producer can be dry and fresh to sweet.

- ☐ **Chianti.** From a blend of grapes this fruity, light ruby-to-garnet-colored red may be called Chianti Riserva when aged three or more years.

- ☐ **Chianti Classico.** From a designated portion of the Chianti wine district. To be labeled Chianti Classico, both vineyard and winery must be within the specified region.

- ☐ **Claret.** British term for red Bordeaux wines.

- ☐ **Colombard.** The second most widely planted white variety in California, nearly all of it for jug wines. It produces an abundant crop, and makes clean and simple wines.

- ☐ **Constantia.** This legendary sweet wine from South Africa, was a favorite of Napoleon. It comes from an estate called Groot Constantia.

- ☐ **Cortese.** White wine grape grown in Piedmont and Lombardy. Best known for the wine, Gavi. The grape produces a light-bodied, crisp, well-balanced wine.

- ☐ **Dolcetto.** From northwest Piedmont it produces soft, round, fruity wines fragrant with licorice and almonds.

- ☐ **Eiswein.** "Ice wine," A sweet German wine, made from grapes that have frozen on the vine. Freezing concentrates the sugars in the grapes prior to harvesting.

- ☐ **Frascati.** An Italian fruity, golden white wine, may be dry to sweet.

- ☐ **Gamay.** Beaujolais makes its famous, fruity reds exclusively from one of the many Gamays available. Low in alcohol and relatively high in acidity, the wines are meant to be drunk soon after bottling; whipped onto shelves everywhere almost overnight.

- ☐ **Gamay Beaujolais.** Primarily used for blending.

- ☐ **Gattinara.** A Piedmont red made from Nebbiolo blended with other grapes. Powerful and long-lived.

- ☐ **Gewürztraminer.** A distinctive floral bouquet & spicy flavor are hallmarks of this medium-sweet wine. Grown mainly in Alsace region of France & Germany.

- ☐ **Grappa.** Italian spirit distilled from pomace. Dry and high in alcohol, an after-dinner drink.

- ☐ **Grenache.** Used for blending and making of Rose in California, while in France it is blended to make Chateauneuf-du-Pape. Originally from Spain, the second most widely grown grape in the world. It produces a fruity, spicy, medium-bodied wine.

- ☐ **Kir.** An aperitif from the Burgundy Region of France. A glass of dry white wine and a teaspoon of crème de cassis make this popular drink.

- ☐ **Lambrusco.** A fizzy, usually red, dry to sweet wine from northern Italy.

- ☐ **Liebfraumilch.** A blended German white, semisweet and fairly neutral, which accounts for up to 50 percent of all German wine exports.

- ☐ **Madeira.** A fortified wine named for the island on which its grapes are grown. The wine is slowly heated in a storeroom to over 110°F, and allowed to cool over a period of months. Styles range from dry apéritifs, from the Sercial grape, to rich and sweet Boal and Malmsey.

- ☐ **Malbec.** This not-very-hardy grape has been steadily replaced by Merlot and the two Cabernets. However, Argentina is markedly successful with this varietal. In the United States Malbec is a blending grape only.

- ☐ **Marc.** A distilled spirit made from pomace. Italy calls it grappa; in Burgundy, Marc de Bourgogne; in Champagne, Marc de Champagne. Dry and high in alcohol, typically an after-dinner drink.

- ☐ **Marsala.** Made from Grillo, Catarratto, or Inzolia grapes, this Sicilian wine may be dry or sweet and is commonly used in cooking.

- ☐ **Marsanne.** A full-bodied, moderately intense wine with spice, pear and citrus notes. Popular in the Rhône & Australia has some of the world's oldest vineyards. California's "Rhône-Rangers" have had considerable success with this variety.

- ☐ **Mead.** Common in medieval Europe, a wine made by fermenting honey and water. Wine makers now making flavored meads.

- ☐ **Meritage.** Vintners sought to establish standards of identifying red & white wines made of traditional Bordeaux grape blends. The wine must blend two or more Bordeaux grape varieties. Have less than 90% of any single variety. Be limited to a max of 25,000 cases produced.

- ☐ **Merlot.** Herbs, Green Olive, Cherry & Chocolate. Softer & medium in weight with fewer tannins than Cabernet and ready to drink sooner. Takes well to Oak aging.

- ☐ **Montepulciano.** A medium to full-bodied wine, with good color and structure.
- ☐ **Mourvedre.** A pleasing wine, of medium-weight, with spicy cherry and berry flavors and moderate tannins. Often used in Châteauneuf-du-Pape.
- ☐ **Müller-Thurgau.** A cross of two grapes, Sylvaner and Riesling. Mainly grown in Germany, Northern Italy, and New Zealand. Light in color, and can be dry to medium dry.
- ☐ **Muscat.** Also known as Muscat Blanc and Muscat Canelli. With pronounced spice and floral it can also be used for blending. A versatile grape that can turn into anything from Asti Spumante and Muscat de Canelli to a dry wine like Muscat d'Alsace. Famously called Moscato.
- ☐ **Nebbiolo.** The great grape of Northern Italy, which excels there in Barolo and Barbaresco. The wines are light and uncomplicated, bearing no resemblance to the Italian types.
- ☐ **Petit Verdot.** Used for blending with Cabernet Sauvignon.
- ☐ **Petite Sirah.** Plum & blackberry flavors mark this deep, ruby colored wine. Usually full-bodied with chewy tannins. Used in France & California as a blending wine.
- ☐ **Pinot Blanc.** Similar flavor and texture to Chardonnay it is used in Champagne, Burgundy, and Alsace. It can be intense, and complex, with ripe pear, spice, citrus and honey notes.
- ☐ **Pinot Grigio/Pinot Gris.** At its best this varietal produces wines that are soft, perfumed with more color than most other white wines. Grown mainly in northeast Italy, but as Pinot Gris it is grown in Alsace & known as Tokay.
- ☐ **Pinot Meunier.** Grown in the Champagne region of France, it is blended with Pinot Noir and Chardonnay to add fruit flavors to champagne.
- ☐ **Pinot Noir.** Difficult to grow but at its best it is smooth & richer than Cabernet Sauvignon with less tannin. Raisin like flavors with undertones of black cherry, spice & raspberry.
- ☐ **Pinotage.** A cross between Pinot Noir and Cinsault. Grown in South Africa. Fermented at higher temperatures and aged in new oak for finesse and wonderful berry flavors.
- ☐ **Port.** Fortified wine from the Douro region of Portugal. Styles include: Late Bottle (LB), Tawny, Ruby, Aged, and Vintage. Mostly sweet and red.
- ☐ **Retsina.** Dry white Greek wine flavored with pine resin. It is an acquired taste. Dominant flavor is turpentine. Riesling Flavors of apricot & tropical fruit with floral aromas are characteristics of this widely varying wine. Styles range from dry to sweet.
- ☐ **Riesling.** Riesling is a white grape variety which originated in the Rhine region. It is an aromatic grape variety displaying flowery, almost perfumed, aromas as well as high acidity.
- ☐ **Rosé.** Sometimes called blush. Any light pink wine, dry to sweet, made by removing the skins of red grapes early in the fermentation process or by mixing red and white.
- ☐ **Roussanne.** A white wine grape of the northern Rhône Valley, mainly for blending with the white wine grape Marsanne.
- ☐ **Sangiovese.** Known for its supple texture, medium to full-bodied spice flavors, raspberry cherry & anise. Sangiovese is used in many fine Italian wines including Chianti.

- ☐ **Sauterns.** A blend of mostly Sémillon and Sauvignon Blanc grapes, affected by Botrytis cinerea, which concentrates the wine's sweetness and alcohol.

- ☐ **Sauvignon Blanc.** Grassy & herbaceous flavors and aromas mark this light and medium-bodied wine, sometimes with hints of gooseberry & black currant. Also labeled Fume Blanc.

- ☐ **Sémillon.** The foundation of Sauternes, and many of the dry whites of Graves and Pessac-Léognan. It can make a wonderful late-harvest wine, with complex fig, pear, tobacco and honey notes. As a blending wine it adds body, flavor and texture to Sauvignon Blanc.

- ☐ **Sherry.** Fortified wine from the Jerez de la Frontera district in southern Spain. Palomino is the main grape variety, with Pedro Ximénez used for the sweeter, heavier wines. Drier Sherries are best served chilled; the medium-sweet to sweet are best at room temperature.

- ☐ **Soave.** A straw-colored dry white wine Italy's Veneto Region. In 1948, the Muscat of Alexandria and Grenache Gris grapes were combined to create this delicate Muscat flavor.

- ☐ **Trebbiano.** Trebbiano in Italy and Ugni Blanc in France. Found in almost any basic white Italian wine, and actually a sanctioned ingredient of the blend used for Chianti. In France, it is often called St. Émilion, and used for Cognac and Armagnac brandy.

- ☐ **Valpolicella.** A light, semidry red from Italy's Veneto Region, typically drunk young.

- ☐ **Verdicchio.** Italian white that produces a pale, light-bodied, crisp wine.

- ☐ **Viognier.** Viognier, is one of the most difficult grapes to grow. It makes a floral and spicy white wine, medium to full-bodied and very fruity, with apricot and peach aromas.

- ☐ **Zinfandel.** With predominant raspberry flavors and a spicy aroma, Zinfandels can be bold and intense as well as light and fruity. It takes well to blending bringing out flavors of cherry, wild berry & plum with notes of leather, earth & tar.

Restaurants to Eat at Before You Die

This list comes from the late great Anthony Bourdain, who was an American celebrity chef, author, journalist, and travel documentarian. He starred in programs focusing on the exploration of international culture, cuisine, and the human condition.

- ☐ St. John – London
- ☐ El Bulli – Girona, Spain
- ☐ The French Laundry – Napa Valley, CA
- ☐ Per Se – New York City
- ☐ Sin Huat Eating House – Singapore
- ☐ Le Bernardin – New York
- ☐ Salumi – Seattle
- ☐ Russ & Daughters – New York
- ☐ Katz's Delicatessen – New York
- ☐ Etxebarri – Axpe, Spain
- ☐ Sukiyabashi Jiro – Tokyo
- ☐ Hot Doug's – Chicago
- ☐ Oklahoma Joe's Barbecue – Kansas City

Other Restaurants to Eat at Before You Die

- ☐ _____
- ☐ _____
- ☐ _____
- ☐ _____
- ☐ _____
- ☐ _____
- ☐ _____
- ☐ _____
- ☐ _____
- ☐ _____
- ☐ _____
- ☐ _____
- ☐ _____
- ☐ _____
- ☐ _____
- ☐ _____
- ☐ _____
- ☐ _____
- ☐ _____
- ☐ _____
- ☐ _____
- ☐ _____
- ☐ _____
- ☐ _____
- ☐ _____
- ☐ _____
- ☐ _____
- ☐ _____
- ☐ _____
- ☐ _____

Bars in America to Drink at before you die

We have all been to the occasional dive bar. We don't go there because we know it's good, we go there to have a good time. I love bars with a good ambiance and fun creative ways to drink and to have a great time.

- ☐ Good Times at Davey Wayne's - Los Angeles, California
- ☐ No Vacancy - Hollywood, California
- ☐ The View Lounge - San Francisco, California
- ☐ The Tunnel Bar - North Hampton Massachusetts
- ☐ The Carousel Bar - New Orleans, Louisiana
- ☐ Please Don't Tell - New York, New York
- ☐ Minus 5 Ice Bar - Las Vegas, Nevada
- ☐ The Signature Lounge - Chicago, Illinois
- ☐ Percy's and Co. - Seattle, Washington
- ☐ The Unicorn Bar - Seattle, Washington
- ☐ Clockwork - Raleigh, North Carolina
- ☐ The Laundry Room - Las Vegas Nevada
- ☐ The Way Station - Brooklyn, New York
- ☐ Punch Bowl Social - Denver, Colorado
- ☐ Secrets - Ocean City, Maryland
- ☐ Noble Experiment - San Diego, California
- ☐ Manifesto - Kansas City, Missouri
- ☐ The Safe House - Milwaukee, Wisconsin
- ☐ Founding Fathers Pub - Buffalo, New York

Other Bars I want to Visit

Be One with Nature

The Most Beautiful Trees in the World

I saw this post on Facebook the other day of all these beautiful and obscure trees we have probably never seen and I was like I have to put this in my book. Trust me, these trees are magnificent. They have a beauty I never thought possible, and some seem to look out of this world.

- ☐ **125+ Year Old Rhododendron "Tree", Canada.** This huge 125-year-old rhododendron is technically not a tree – most are considered to be shrubs.
- ☐ **144-Year-Old Wisteria, Japan.** At 1,990 square meters (about half an acre), this huge wisteria is the largest of its kind in Japan.
- ☐ **Wind-Swept Trees, New Zealand.** These trees on Slope Point, the southern tip of New Zealand, grow at an angle because they're constantly buffeted by extreme Antarctic winds.
- ☐ **Beautiful Japanese Maple in Portland, Oregon.**
- ☐ **Antarctic Beech Draped in Hanging Moss, Oregon.** The Antarctic beech is native to Chile and Argentina, though this specimen is from the United States' North Pacific region.
- ☐ **Blooming Cherry Trees in Bonn, Germany.** This beautiful tunnel of cherry blossoms blooms in Bonn, Germany in April.
- ☐ **Angel Oak in John's Island, South Carolina.** The Angel Oak in South Carolina stands 66.5 ft (20 m) tall and is estimated to be more than 1400 or 1500 years old.
- ☐ **Flamboyant Tree, Brazil.** The flamboyant tree is endemic to Madagascar, but it grows in tropical areas around the world.
- ☐ **Dragon's blood Trees, Yemen.** This tree earned its fearsome name due to its crimson red sap, which is used as a dye and was used as a violin varnish, an alchemical ingredient, and a folk remedy for various ailments.
- ☐ **The President, Third-Largest Giant Sequoia, California.** Located in Sequoia National Park in California, it stands 241 ft (73m) tall and has a ground circumference of 93 ft (28m). It is the third largest giant sequoia in the world (second if you count its branches in addition to its trunk).
- ☐ **Maple Tree Tunnel, Oregon.**
- ☐ **Rainbow Eucalyptus Kauai, Hawaii.** The rainbow eucalyptus, which grows throughout the South Pacific, is both useful and beautiful. It is prized for both the colorful patches left by its shedding bark and for its pulpwood, which is used to make paper.
- ☐ **Jacarandas in Cullinan, South Africa.** These beautiful Jacarandas, with their violet flowers, are native to Latin America and the Caribbean.
- ☐ **Avenue of Oaks at Dixie Plantation, South Carolina.** This avenue of oak trees was planted sometime in the 1790s on Dixie Plantation in South Carolina.

- ☐ **Baobab Trees, Madagascar.** These baobabs in Madagascar are excellent at storing water in their thick trunks to use during droughts.
- ☐ **The Dark Hedges, Northern Ireland.** Ireland's Dark Hedges were planted in the 18th century. This stunning beech tree tunnel was featured on Game of Thrones as well.

Other Trees to Visit

☐ _____
☐ _____
☐ _____
☐ _____
☐ _____
☐ _____
☐ _____
☐ _____
☐ _____
☐ _____
☐ _____
☐ _____
☐ _____
☐ _____
☐ _____
☐ _____
☐ _____
☐ _____
☐ _____
☐ _____
☐ _____
☐ _____
☐ _____
☐ _____
☐ _____

☐ _____
☐ _____
☐ _____
☐ _____
☐ _____
☐ _____
☐ _____
☐ _____
☐ _____
☐ _____
☐ _____
☐ _____
☐ _____
☐ _____
☐ _____
☐ _____
☐ _____
☐ _____
☐ _____
☐ _____
☐ _____
☐ _____
☐ _____
☐ _____
☐ _____

Most Beautiful Gardens in the World

I am all about surrounding yourself with the beauty that is nature. It has a calming effect and grounds you. If you are a spiritual person, you spend a lot of time outside and enjoying the abundance that nature has to offer. It is good for your mental health to spend at least twenty minutes a day outside. Fun fact as per usual.

- ☐ **Kenroku-en, Kanazawa, Japan.** In designing their works, Japanese gardeners seek to create an ideal landscape within a particular space. Kenroku-en is considered to be one of the finest examples of Japanese gardens, built over the course of 200 years starting in the mid-17th century.

- ☐ **Keukenhof, Lisse, Netherlands.** Covering nearly 80 acres, Keukenhof is one of the largest flower gardens in the world. With all that land comes a lot of bulbs—about seven million are planted each year for a spectacular spring blossom. The garden is only open between March and May. You'll also find plenty of tulips, which the country is known for.

- ☐ **Nong Nooch Tropical Botanical Garden, Pattaya, Thailand.** In 1954 Pisit and Nongnooch Tansacha purchased 600 acres of land on which they planned to build a fruit plantation, but they decided to dedicate the grounds to conservation. In 1980 they opened their tropical garden to the public.

- ☐ **Gardens of Versailles, Versailles, France.** A list of top gardens would not be complete without mentioning the gardens of the Château of Versailles. Covering nearly 2,000 acres, the current landscape was designed by gardener André Le Nôtre, who was commissioned by Louis XIV in 1661.

- ☐ **Kew Royal Botanic Gardens, Kew, United Kingdom.** More than just a scenic greenspace, Kew is an internationally renowned research institution, employing hundreds of scientists and researchers. The gardens are home to more than 40,000 species of plants, as well as dozens of historic buildings, including the Victorian-era Palm House.

- ☐ **Brooklyn Botanic Gardens, New York, New York.** It's not often you find a 52-acre garden in the heart of a major metropolis, but that's exactly what you'll find thanks to the Brooklyn Botanic Garden. The garden is known for its 200 cherry trees, which take center stage during a month-long blossom festival.

- ☐ **Jardin Majorelle, Marrakech, Morocco.** French painter Jacques Majorelle spent four decades crafting his beloved garden around his villa in Marrakech. Noted for the luminous blue paint on its buildings, gates, pots and more, the garden was purchased by Yves Saint Laurent and Pierre Bergé in 1980.

- ☐ **Kirstenbosch National Botanical Garden, Cape Town, South Africa.** Established in 1913, the grand Kirstenbosch sits on the slopes of Table Mountain and is dedicated to preserving

South African flora. While the garden comprises nearly 90 acres itself, it is part of a 1,300-acre nature reserve.

☐ **Villa d'Este, Tivoli, Italy.** This 16th-century villa, whose main building is also a marvel, is home to an incredible garden that has 51 fountains. Considering each run on gravity alone, that's a pretty impressive feat. The terraced landscape was the inspiration for many European gardens to follow.

☐ **Summer Palace, Beijing, China.** A combination of historic pavilions, temples, bridges, and a hilly natural landscape, the Summer Palace was deemed a "masterpiece of Chinese landscape garden design" by UNESCO, which designated it a World Heritage Site in 1998. Sidenote, flora filled garden seriously calls for a cute sun hat… it's almost a rule.

☐ **Monet's Gardens, Giverny, France.** If you visit one garden in your life, let it be this one. Claude Monet's garden, at the home he lived in in Giverny, France, is, quite literally, like something out of a painting. A quick train ride away from Paris, the garden is split into two parts - a flower garden called Clos Normand and a Japanese-inspired water garden.

☐ **Koishikawa Korakuen Gardens, Tokyo.** This 17th Century garden was created in 1629 by Mito Yorifusa and completed by his son. It incorporates both Chinese and Japanese elements.

☐ **Volksgarten, Vienna, Austria.** This garden was laid out by Ludwig Remy in 1821 and is situated on the grounds of Hofburg Palace. It's famous for its rose garden with over 3,000 rose bushes and 200 different cultivars of roses.

☐ **Longwood Gardens, Pennsylvania, USA.** These gardens cover an impressive 1,077 acres, woodlands and meadows. The gardens came to fruition after Pierre S. du Pont purchased them in 1906 and have been wow-ing visitors ever since.

☐ **Giardini Botanici Villa Taranto, Piedmont, Italy.** These gardens were established between 1931 and 1940 when a new owner completely transformed the gardens of Villa Taranto into the floral oasis that exists today.

☐ **Château de Villandry, France.** Located in Villandry in central France, this Chateau is known for its spectacularly manicured gardens. The chateau was purchased in 1906 by Joachim Carvallo who spent a large amount of time curating the extravagant gardens.

☐ **Arundel Castle Gardens, UK.** In the grounds of Arundel Castle, you will find these picturesque gardens and each April and May over 60,000 tulips bloom. Better yet, it's just an hour and a half train ride from London.

☐ **Las Pozas, Mexico.** Located more than 2,000 feet above sea level, this garden is filled with surrealist structures, created by eccentric English poet Edward James, in a subtropical rainforest. Natural waterfalls are interlaced with pools and the towering structures.

☐ **Butchart Gardens, Canada.** Located in Canada's British Columbia district, these gardens receive over a million visitors each year - and for good reason. A designated National Historic Site of Canada they contain over 900 varieties of plants that bloom March through October.

☐ **Humble Administrator's Garden, China.** These gardens are over a thousand years old and consist of a labyrinthine of connected islands. A bit like a Chinese water village.

- ☐ **San Grato Park, Switzerland.** Located above Lake Lugano, you can wander through one of the five themed paths – including the aptly named 'Fairytale Trail'.

- ☐ **Crathes Castle, Scotland.** The walled gardens of this 16th Century Tower House have been perfected over the last four centuries and include an array of stunning florals.

- ☐ **Royal Botanic Gardens, Melbourne, Australia.** Located on the banks of the Yarra river in Melbourne is one of the fascinating gardens in Australia, Discover the rare and beautiful plants, breathtaking landscapes and iconic buildings in the garden.

- ☐ **Desert Botanical Garden, Phoenix, Arizona, US.** The 140-acre Desert Botanical Garden in Phoenix, Arizona has the world's finest collection of arid-land plants from deserts around the world in a unique outdoor setting. The Garden also offers a variety of lectures and workshops on desert landscaping and horticulture, botanical art and illustration, nature art and photography, and health. The Garden has more than 50,000 accessioned plants throughout its five thematic trails.

- ☐ **The Garden of Cosmic Speculation, Scotland.** It is a private garden built by Charles Jencks and his late wife Maggie in Portrack House inspired science and mathematics, with sculptures and landscaping on these themes, such as Black Holes and Fractals. One of the beautiful abstract gardens you will ever see.

- ☐ **Stourhead Warminster, England.** Stourhead is the best example of a garden inspired by the great landscape and reason enough to visit England. The gardens incorporate the ever-changing vistas around a lake. The Arcadian ideal is the sort of background scene you see in many Italian Renaissance portraits, including the Mona Lisa.

More Beautiful Gardens to Visit

☐ _____	☐ _____
☐ _____	☐ _____
☐ _____	☐ _____
☐ _____	☐ _____
☐ _____	☐ _____
☐ _____	☐ _____
☐ _____	☐ _____
☐ _____	☐ _____
☐ _____	☐ _____
☐ _____	☐ _____
☐ _____	☐ _____
☐ _____	☐ _____

Best Hikes to Basic Yourself

We have all been there. Being called basic, isn't fun, it's a lifestyle. Basic isn't bad. I love to hike, I don't, however, like pumpkin spice lattes or Lululemon yoga paints. I prefer Alo Yoga and mocha frappes from McDonalds.

- ☐ The Narrows, USA
- ☐ Pays Dogon, Mali
- ☐ The Haute Route, France & Switzerland
- ☐ GR20, France
- ☐ Inca Trail, Machu Picchu, Peru
- ☐ Everest Base Camp, Nepal
- ☐ Overland Track, Australia
- ☐ Routeburn Track, New Zealand
- ☐ Baltoro Glacier and K2, Pakistan
- ☐ Fitz Roy Trek, Argentina
- ☐ Cinque Terre, Italy
- ☐ Santa Cruz Trek, Peru
- ☐ Torres del Paine Circuit, Chile
- ☐ Desert Trek to Petra, Jordan
- ☐ Kungsleden, Sweden
- ☐ West Coast Trail, Canada
- ☐ Sarek National Park, Sweden
- ☐ Muliwai Trail, Hawaii
- ☐ Croagh Patrick, Ireland
- ☐ Grindelwald, Switzerland
- ☐ Appalachian Trail, USA
- ☐ Zillertal Alps, Austria
- ☐ North Drakensberg Traverse, South Africa
- ☐ Cape Wrath Trail, Scotland
- ☐ Simien Mountain National Park, Ethiopia
- ☐ Polar Route, Greenland
- ☐ Kalalau Trail, Hawaii
- ☐ Cordillera Apolobamba, Bolivia
- ☐ Grand Canyon Rim-to-Rim Hike
- ☐ Yosemite Grand Traverse
- ☐ Bay of Fires, Australia
- ☐ Long Range traverse, Newfoundland, Canada
- ☐ Queen Charlotte Track, New Zealand
- ☐ West Coast Trail, British Columbia
- ☐ Tour Du Mont Blanc, France/Italy/Switzerland
- ☐ Bibbulmun Track, Australia
- ☐ Tongariro Alpine Crossings, New Zealand
- ☐ Overland Track, New Zealand
- ☐ Scottish National Park
- ☐ Sierra High Route
- ☐ Arctic Circle Trail
- ☐ Dolomites, Italy
- ☐ La Ciudad Perdida, Columbia
- ☐ Hadrian's Wall Path

- ☐ Israel National Trail, Israel
- ☐ Great Ocean Walk, Victoria, Australia
- ☐ Otter Trail, South Africa
- ☐ Chilkoot Trail, Canada
- ☐ Tonquin Valley, Alberta, Canada
- ☐ Berliner Höhenweg

Other Hikes to Basic Yourself

☐ _____
☐ _____
☐ _____
☐ _____
☐ _____
☐ _____
☐ _____
☐ _____
☐ _____
☐ _____
☐ _____
☐ _____
☐ _____
☐ _____
☐ _____
☐ _____
☐ _____
☐ _____
☐ _____
☐ _____
☐ _____
☐ _____
☐ _____
☐ _____
☐ _____
☐ _____
☐ _____
☐ _____

☐ _____
☐ _____
☐ _____
☐ _____
☐ _____
☐ _____
☐ _____
☐ _____
☐ _____
☐ _____
☐ _____
☐ _____
☐ _____
☐ _____
☐ _____
☐ _____
☐ _____
☐ _____
☐ _____
☐ _____
☐ _____
☐ _____
☐ _____
☐ _____
☐ _____
☐ _____
☐ _____
☐ _____

Randomness Not Included

Extra Pages

References

Donnelly, M. (2016) *The Ultimate Single Girl Bucket List: 61 Dates You Can Take Your Beautiful Self on This Year*. Thought Catalog. https://thoughtcatalog.com/marisa-donnelly/2016/12/the-ultimate-single-girl-bucket-list-61-dates-you-can-take-your-beautiful-self-on-this-year/

Lyons, S. (2018). *The Summer Bucket List for Single Girls Who Just Wanna Have Fun.* Elite Daily. https://www.elitedaily.com/p/the-summer-bucket-list-for-single-girls-who-just-wanna-have-fun-8882347

Tee. *The Ultimate Single Girl Bucket List.* Pucker Mob. https://puckermob.com/moblog/the-ultimate-single-girl-bucket-list/

Meanley, E. (2010). *36 Things Every Single Girl Must Do Before She Settles Down.* Glamour. https://www.glamour.com/story/36-things-every-single-girl-mu

Volpone, E. (2016). *Ultimate Bucket List for Singles.* Odyssey. https://www.theodysseyonline.com/ultimate-bucket-list-singles

Oerman, A. (2014). *11 Places You Need to Have Sex.* Women's Health Magazine. https://www.womenshealthmag.com/sex-and-love/a19959488/places-you-need-to-have-sex/

Riordan, H. (2016). *50 Hot Places to Have Sex if You're Adventurous as Fuck.* Thought Catalog. https://thoughtcatalog.com/holly-riordan/2016/06/50-hot-places-to-have-sex-if-youre-adventurous-as-fuck/

Neakon. (2019). *200 Best Places Ever to Have Sex.* Paired Life. https://pairedlife.com/physical-intimacy/150-Best-Places-Ever-to-Have-Sex

Lauren. (2020). *My 100 Best Travel Tips from Ten Years of Travel.* Never Ending Footsteps. https://www.neverendingfootsteps.com/100-best-travel-tips/

Matt. (2018). *By Best 61 Travel Tips to Make You the World's Savviest Traveler.* Nomadic Matt. https://www.nomadicmatt.com/travel-blogs/61-travel-tips/

Karsten, M. (2020). *My 50 Best Travel Tips After 10 Years Traveling the World.* Expert Vagabond. https://expertvagabond.com/best-travel-tips/

Karsten, M. (2020). *25 Important Travel Safety Tips Everyone Should Know.* Expert Vagabond. https://expertvagabond.com/travel-safety-tips/

The Claim Compass Blog. (2019). *50 Tips from Experts on Ways to Make Money Traveling.* https://www.claimcompass.eu/blog/make-money-traveling/

Derek. (2013). *42 Ways You can Make Money and Travel the World.* Wandering Earl. https://www.wanderingearl.com/42-ways-you-can-make-money-and-travel-the-world/

D, Lina. (2014). *16 of the Most Magnificent Trees in the World.* Bored Panda. https://www.boredpanda.com/most-beautiful-trees/?utm_source=google&utm_medium=organic&utm_campaign=organic

Other Books by Sarah Melland

THE BREAKUP BAND AID/THE BREAKUP BAND AID WORKBOOK
This "How Not To" book gives you everything you supposedly need in a breakup book. Plus, helpful insights as to how not to have a nervous breakdown or a restraining order. It will make you laugh out loud, cry uncontrollable tears, get in shape, travel around the world, and make you glow like the shining confident person you were always meant to be.

PRACTICING LOVE/JOURNAL EDITION
Practicing Love will help you meditate with ease, turn your mind off to distractions, and open your world of possibilities with easy tips you can incorporate into your everyday busy life. It goes into depth about how the ego makes you operate out of fear and shows you how to turn that negative mindset into one that empowers you to conquer obstacles by getting out of your comfort zone. It goes through simple descriptions of all the universal laws that will help you live a more positive, happy, and fulfilled life. It gives you hundreds of affirmations you can recite when you are feeling down in any scenario. It will also show you which words you need to eliminate from your vocabulary immediately and how to start talking in manifestation mode 24/7. It has tons of exercises to help you live in the present moment, become more patient, support yourself in forgiving yourself and others, become less selfish, not react out of judgement, and finally, to always feel unconditionally loved.

PRACTICING LOVE GRATITUDE JOURNAL
Practicing Love Gratitude Journal is 365 days of writing prompts that will take you through all the spiritual laws of attraction and how to show grace in your everyday lives. It allows you to go deep within yourself through daily reflection, shows you what you have been resisting and teaches you how to flip the switch. It will help you heal on numerous levels, relieve stress, anxiety, self-doubt, and ultimately aid in conquering your fears through forgiveness and perseverance. You will create easy, attainable every day goals by setting your intentions and maximizing manifestation throughout the day. You will also learn how to break free from your ego mindset, discover your self-worth, and realize what a truly magical person you really are. May your life be filled with the vibration of love, and always remember to write from a place of gratitude.

A SINGLE GIRL'S GUIDE TO HILARIOUS FACTS YOU NEVER KNEW ABOUT SEX
Have you ever wondered how many different types of kisses there are? The history of condoms? Fun facts about penises and vaginas? When sex toys were invented? Are you nodding your head to all these questions? If so, this is the book for you. Every single woman should have useless sex facts in her repertoire. There's even a masturbation playlist for you to get your freak on and ride high for hours. Anything you could possibly want to know is in this book. Fun Fact: Cleopatra invented the dildo using an empty gourd and stuffed it full of angry bees. She is now my spirit animal. Tip: Sperm can be considered an anti-aging treatment, as it has a tightening effect on the skin. I am only going to try this one time, and then I'm out. Plus, thousands upon thousands of other craziness that goes with everything sex. You will never have a dead air conversation after reading this book.

Instagram: @yourdatingunexpert
www.sarahmelland.com

www.ingramcontent.com/pod-product-compliance
Lightning Source LLC
Chambersburg PA
CBHW081106080526
44587CB00021B/3467